September 29, 1980

TO WHOM IT MAY CONCERN:

Re:  Mary S. Relfe
     Montgomery, Alabama   36104

..."A most valued client of First Alabama Bank.
I would not hesitate to enter into any venture
with her that she considers to be sound.

...I have watched her grow in the various business ventures that she is in, all of which, I
might add, have been most successful.

As to her character and personal habits, I
can attest to them being impeccable.

I feel that I have gained much more from
knowing Mrs. Relfe these past sixteen years
than she has ever gained from the advice
that I have given to her."

**Excerpts taken from letter of Mr. Jack Eley, Senior Vice
President, First Alabama Bank, Montgomery, Alabama.**

# WHEN YOUR MONEY FAILS ⑥⑥⑥

## the "666 System" is here.

Mary Stewart Relfe, Ph.D.

First printing — January, 1981
Sixteenth printing — August, 1982

ISBN 0-9607-986-0-9

Copyright © 1981 by Ministries, Inc.
P.O. Box 4038
Montgomery, Alabama 36104
U.S.A.

*Printed in the United States of America*

# DEDICATION

To my beloved husband,
the late Conyers Blakely Relfe, M.D.
May 9, 1919 — January 25, 1978

and

To my beloved Heavenly Bridegroom,
who "passed by me,
and looked upon me
and the time was the time of love;
and He spread His skirt over me . . .
and sware unto me,
and entered into a covenant with me,
and I became His."
Ezekiel 16:8

v

# APPRECIATION

I am deeply indebted to many prophetic ministries, from whose writings I have gleaned over the years, and in many instances, whose words became my words as I taught, and subsequently as I wrote. I sincerely pray that I have avoided the dreaded boundary line of plagiarism.

- SOUTHWEST RADIO CHURCH, P.O. Box 1144, Oklahoma City, Oklahoma 73101, Dr. David Webber, Pastor. And, to Dr. Emil Gaverluk, Staff Member, my special thanks.

- DR. JACK VAN IMPE, Box J, Royal Oak, Michigan 48068, who so unselfishly shared his research with me. Bless you, Jack.

- THE REV. COLIN HOYLE DEAL, End Time News, Christ Returns by 1988, P.O. Box 455, Rutherford College, North Carolina 28671, whose encouragement came at a critical time.

- **THE REV. SIMON PETER CAMERON,** Founder/President, New Hope Bible College (Faith Acres), Peterhead, Scotland, an acknowledged scholar, who laboriously critiqued the manuscript and proofed the book. God bless you, Simon.

- **BERNARD STEWART,** my brother, who was my "strong arm" during the "desert days" of my life; the days following the loss of my only child, a 27-year-old son, Anthony, my son, my son, whose untimely death came in the midst of this research!

- **SALLY O'BRIEN,** the friend closer than a brother, without whose prayers, encouragement, patience, and daily assistance, this work would have never been completed.

# GRACIOUS ACKNOWLEDGMENTS

for permission to quote from their copyrighted material:

- *ZONDERVAN PUBLISHING HOUSE.* For quotes from *Explore The Book,* by J. Sidlow Baxter.

- *EERDMANS PUBLISHING COMPANY.* For quotes from *Systematic Theology,* by Charles Hodge.

- *BOOK DIGEST.* For quotes from *In Search of Identity,* by Anwar L. Sadat; and *Free to Choose,* by Milton Freedman.

- *SCHOLASTIC MAGAZINE, INC.* For quotes from *Public Needs and Private Rights — Who is Watching You?* Also, for reproduction of cover of September 20, 1973.

- Artwork by Gene Beck

- Book title by Bernard Stewart

- Photograph of author by Linda White

# BULLETIN OF
# THE ATOMIC SCIENTISTS
## January 1981

"We feel impelled to record and to emphasize the accelerating drift toward disaster in almost all realms of social activity. Accordingly, we have decided to move the hands of the Bulletin's Clock — symbol of the world's approach to nuclear doomsday — forward from seven to four minutes before midnight."

*Each minute represents a year. Midnight represents nuclear disaster.*

Why does this elite but secular group of scientists know more about the end of the age than the Church?

"The children of this world are wiser . . . than the children of light."

Luke 16:8

INTRODUCTION

# "THE BIG THREE" PROPHETIC FULFILLMENTS OF THIS AGE

1.  The birth of Jesus Christ in 3 B.C.
    Isaiah 9:6, Micah 5:2; Seventh Century B.C.

2.  The Declaration of the Nation of Israel, May 14, 1948, and subsequent capture of Jerusalem in 1967 by the Jews.
    Luke 21:24; First Century A.D.

3.  The world wide usage of the number "666," the numerical entity characterizing and identifying the Last One World Government, 1980.
    Revelation 13:18; First Century A.D.

This book is about the third most significant prophetic fulfillment of this age; the sudden emergence of the usage, nationally and internationally, of the number "666" by political, economic, and religious institutions of the world, now forming the conglomerate One World Government, destined to control all peoples and nations the last seven years of this age.

# TABLE OF CONTENTS

# CHAPTER I

*"Here is a puzzle that calls for careful thought to solve it. Let those who are able, interpret this code: the numerical values of the letters in his name add to 666!"*

REVELATION 13:18 LB

# "666"
# ITS SUDDEN
# WORLDWIDE USAGE

It was not the design of the floor tile made here in the United States and purchased locally in Montgomery, Alabama, that almost mesmerized me, it was the bold prefix "666" stamped on both sides! I had just filed a photograph of a man's dress shirt manufactured in China and purchased in the United States with the number "666" on the label. Before closing the folder, I gazed at the 8x10 glossy which AP Wire Photo Service had just mailed to me of the official reopening of the Suez Canal showing the first warship entering the canal carrying on board Egyptian President Anwar Sadat, which had on its bow the big bold numbers "666." My repertoire of recent information concerning the national and international usage of the number "666" was becoming engorged.

The file contains additional information which indicates that:

- World Bank code number is "666."

- Australia's national bank cards have on them "666."

- New credit cards in U.S. are now being assigned the prefix "666."

- Olivetti Computer Systems P6060 use processing numbers beginning with "666."

- Central computers for Sears, Belk, J.C. Penney and Montgomery Ward prefix transactions with "666" as necessitated by computer programs.

- Shoes made in European Common Market Countries have stamped on inside label "666."

- Visa is 6 6 6; Vi, *Roman* Numeral, is 6; the "zz" sound, Zeta, the 6th character in the *Greek* alphabet, is 6; a, *English,* is 6.

- Computers made by Lear Siegler have a seal on the side on which is stamped the number "666."

- Federal Government Medicaid Service Employees Division number is "666."

- IRS Alcohol, Tobacco, and Firearms Division has on their employee badges the number "666."

- IRS Instructions for Non-profit Corporation Employee 1979, W-2 Form requires the prefix "666."

- IRS began to require the prefix "666" on some forms; for example, W-2P, disability is 666.3; death is 666.4, etc., as early as 1977. See p. 248.

- State Governments are now using on their office purchasing paperwork the number "666."

- President Carter's new Secret Security Force patches have on them "666."

Lottery ticket brought back from Israel in March 1981. A national lottery is being conducted in Israel, and printed on EACH LOTTERY TICKET ARE THE NUMBERS "666."

A repugnantly glaring example of the usage of the numerical entity, "666." This is an advertisement of a nationwide contest in Israel, sponsored by the Department of Education. It is designed to "educate," prepare and condition the Jews to accept "666," which will be the number of their "False Messiah" (the Antichrist), and his World Government System. *Jerusalem Post*, November 25, 1980.

"U.S. Treasury Department, Internal Revenue Service, Alcohol Tobacco and Firearms" Badge. The number "666" is at the bottom.

- The McGregor Clothing Company recently introduced its new "666" Collection of menswear.
- A midwestern telephone company's credit card is encoded "666."
- Identification tags on all foreign made Japanese parts for the Caterpillar Company, Peoria, Illinois, contain the code "666."
- Work gloves manufactured by the Boss Glove Company are stamped "666."
- The Crow's Hybrid Corn Company of Nevada, Iowa, offers a "666" seed as its top yielding hybrid.
- A "new improved" fertilizer, Scotty's "666."

- Tanks built by Chrysler Corporation for President Carter's Secret Security Force have on their sides "666."

- South Central Bell's new Telco Credit Union Cards require the prefix "666," then the person's social security number.

- Metric rulers distributed in 1979 throughout the U.S. have in center the number "666."

- Some financial institutions in Florida are using the number "666."

- ID tags on 1979 GM cars produced in Flint, Michigan contain the number "666."

- The films, Omen I and II concern themselves with a world dictator and the number "666."

- United States Selective Service Cards have on them "666."

- Computer receipts all over the U.S. have on them a group of gray dots surrounding the number "666."

- Overseas telephone operator number from Israel is "666."

- Arab-owned vehicles in Jerusalem have license plates prefixed with "666."

- Record album released by a rock group, Black Sabbath, is named "666."

- Elementary algebra book is entitled "666 Jellybeans."

- Some IBM supermarket equipment is prefixed with the number 3 — "666."

- JC Penney began prefixing account numbers in August, 1980, with "666."

- MasterCard began using on their August, 1980, statements "66."

- Formula for NCR Model 304 Supermarket Computer System is 6 60 6, "666."

- Some US School Systems for Junior High students began using a 6-6-6 System (6 subjects, 6 week report periods, 6 report periods per year).

- Plus numerous other reports of contemporary usage of this number.

- See pictures.

Additionally, some ancient languages used the letters of their alphabet to denote numerical value. Of interest to Bible students are Chaldee, Hebrew, Greek, and Latin, whose letters were used as numbers, as V = 5; X = 10; I = 1 (Roman Numerals).

- Original Latin used only six basic characters to denote numbers . . . these six add up to "666."

- Antiochus IV desecrated the Temple in 168 B.C. Another TYPE of Antichrist, his self-proclaimed title was "God Manifest," in Greek, Epiphaneia. Its numerical value is "666."

- Caesar Nero, another TYPE of Antichrist, in Hebrew is NRON KRS, with a numerical value of

"666."

- The Greek word for "Beast" in Hebrew characters equal "666."

- The Greek word Titan (Titanic in English) in Greek characters is "666."

- $6^2 = 36$; Sum total of all digits in the square of 6 = "666."

- (Number of Man)$^2$ = Sum total of "666."

I stared at the file containing the almost incredible information that had surfaced in the past months on the numerical value of the man's name and institution which will soon be given power over "all kindreds, tongues, and nations"... (the world!). Revelation 13:7. I could only marvel that contained in the ancient languages were many riddles, whose solutions are imperative in properly correlating the past with the present.

The startling reality which everyone must accept is that before the Man, Mr. "666," is "officially" revealed to the world, his institution, characterized by the number "666," must herald the last seven years of this World Age. The Atomic Scientists say it is "T — 4 years" and counting.

The poignant question facing us is how long will it be before we in the United States and the world must use his number "666" with which to buy and sell? Prepare yourself! Hold on to your hat! This is no gimmick! We are already using it! The following chapters will show you why, where, and how you are already using it, even prior to its inscription on your next

Credit Card which is *now ready* to be issued!

No longer can even scoffers say, ''I've heard 'that' all my life.'' Ah, Peter, did they really ask, ''Where now is the promise of His coming? Our Fathers have been laid to their rest, but still everything continues exactly as it has always been since the world began.'' II Peter 3:4 NEB.

I closed the file and began to hum,

> *''Soon and very soon,*
> *We are going to see the King.''*

Lifting my head my eyes caught an inscription on the wall of my study . . . a bold 17th century prediction,

> *''About the Time of the End, a body of men*
> *will be raised up who will turn their attention*
> *to the prophecies, and insist upon their literal*
> *interpretation, in the midst of much clamor*
> *and opposition.''*
>
> Sir Isaac Newton

Ah, John, you were more than a fisherman . . . you were in the Spirit who showed you things to come.

P.S. Sir Isaac, you were more than just a scientist too!

An Arab-owned car in Jerusalem bearing on its license plate the prefix "666." (All Arab-owned vehicles must be prefixed with "666" in order that Israel may quickly identify the enemy in the event of war.) This depicts the "666 System" in Israel.

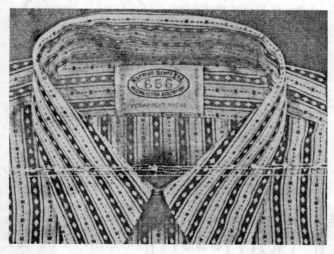

ABOVE: Picture of a shirt made in Red China, with the number "666" on the label forming a trademark. This shirt was sold through a jobber in Hong Kong, and purchased through a retail store in Kansas City, Missouri. (Courtesy of Southwest Radio Church, Oklahoma City.) This depicts the "666 System" emerging in Communist China.

Close-up of shirt labels from Red China.

In his book, *The Next Visitor to Planet Earth,* Dr. Michael Esses describes these labels in shoes made in Italy. This depicts the "666 System" in the European Economic Community.

LSI Computers* made in the U.S. and shipped to Israel have on them this inspection seal. (Courtesy of Dr. Jack Van Impe.) This depicts the "666 System" in the U.S.

*We have been informed officially that LSI has discontinued the usage of "666."

J.C. Penney Card issued in 1980.

Copy of statement from JC Penney.

In addition, Miss O'Brien's Montgomery Ward card (not shown) uses a combination of 6's.

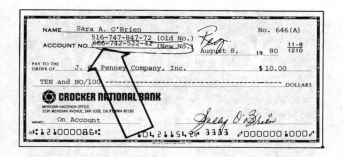

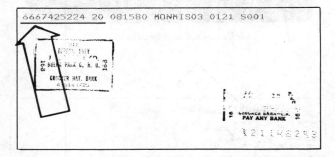

Check paying on account shows old and new numbers. Penney's circled new 666 number as regular number, and endorsed check using the "666 System."

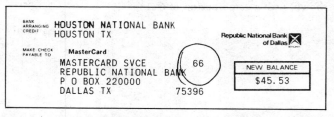

In August, 1980, MasterCharge began their switchover to MasterCard which bears the number "66."

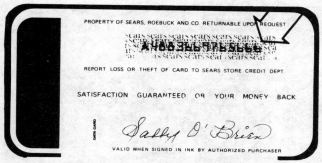

Copy of a 1978 Sears Card which had already begun using the number "666" as a suffix.

The San Francisco Card Center (see upper right) "699." See chapter "The Age of Six," which indicates the sixes are programmed inverted . . . it is still "666."

Also note that on all these account numbers, the initial digit had already been advanced to either 4 or 5.

Copy of section of floor tile, made in the U.S., prefixed on both sides with the number "666." This depicts the "666 System" in the United States Economy.

April 1981, *Ladies Home Journal's* Feature Fiction of the month, "666."

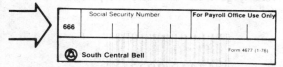

| 666 | Social Security Number | | | For Payroll Office Use Only | | |
|-----|------------------------|--|--|------------------------------|--|--|
| Ⓐ South Central Bell | | | | | Form 4677 (1-76) | |

South Central Bell's Telco Credit Union application.

National Cash Register ad in *Business Week* (4-1980), in which their Financial Terminals (cashless registers) are advertised to replace all the world's outdated currencies pictured. The subtle suggestion is "to operate in this system, we need the World Wide Money Card."

A bank recently gave its customers the perogative of the prefix "666."

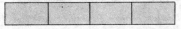

Latest evolution in the Universal Product Code: a horizontal F and H at bottom. On the supermarket receipt was printed, "This UPC is the first sign of the New System." Conjecture: when mark is inserted on body, F = Forehead; H = Hand location.

Financial and government institutions in U.S. and abroad are utilizing variations of this horizontal logo "666."

U. S. NAVY HELICOPTER

U.S. Helicopter "66" which plucked up
Borman, Lovell, and Anders in their
Apollo reentry capsule. This indicates the
"666 System" includes the military hard-
ware of the world. (See Sadat's Warship
"666.") (Artist's rendering.) Courtesy of
*Prophecy Fulfilled in the Fateful Sixties.*
See chapter "The Age of Six," p. 156.

PRESIDENT CARTER'S
SECRET FORCE

President Carter's "Secret Force" tanks
built by Chrysler Corporation with the
number "666" on them.

31

# CHAPTER II

# THE ELECTRONIC (CASHLESS) MONEY SOCIETY

"And he causeth all, both small and great, rich and poor, free and bond, to receive a MARK in their right hand, or in their foreheads: And that no man might buy or sell, save he that had the MARK, or the *name* of the beast, or the NUMBER of his name. Here is wisdom. Let him that hath understanding count the NUMBER of the beast: for it is the NUMBER of a man; and his NUMBER is six hundred threescore and six." Revelation 13:16-18.

Dr. Patrick Fisher: "I think there's one interesting step that we're going to see between now and the rise of the super dictator who will control the economy of the world, and this is the issue of a new credit card. We have gone along quite easily in changing from one card to another, and there's *one more card* to come, and this card is *ready now!* It will be issued to two billion people. This card will be advertised as the best one to have because of its convenience. Everyone must have one. Now you can chop up all your other cards — this replaces all of them."

Dr. Emil Gaverluk: "The scriptures say that anyone who takes the number of the super dictator '666' which will be put on the forehead or hand, will not be allowed to enter the Kingdom of God. What step is that? Is that the next step beyond this card that we are talking about?"

Dr. Fisher: "Yes, it is, it's that close. It's close enough for me to know in my spirit that I don't want this new card when it comes, I will return it."

Dr. Patrick Fisher, Eminent Computer Scientist, Consultant for the Moscow Olympics in 1980; Consultant to Canada Super Conducting Corporation affiliated with McGill University; Consultant to Starsat Canada; being interviewed by Dr. Emil Gaverluk, Ph.D., Ed.D., Scientist and Minister on staff of Southwest Radio Church . . . as broadcast on their network of radio stations, and subsequently on Jewish Voice Broadcast on stations nationwide.

While Americans are buried in a maze of problems concerning the collapsing economy, and the demise of the dollar, we are being quietly, subtly, and dangerously drawn into the Electronic Money Society.

In 1980, a radical and pervasive change surfaced in the issuance of credit cards; a tremendous acceleration in the narrowing down process to the one and final card which will bear each individual's own secret code number micro-encoded in the discretionary data field of Track 2 on the magnetic stripe, which subsequently will be required to be encoded and "marked" in the forehead or right hand.

A Director of Data Processing for a huge banking corporation confided to me in early 1980 that:

1. There was a drastic shift from credit cards to debit cards, with an intermediary step, transaction cards. (The debit card system will result in the total *elimination of credit.*)

2. In 1982, all impressionable machines will become extinct. The information on the front of the card will be meaningless to the transaction. Infra-red scanners will take the pertinent data from the magnetic tape on the back, which *is not visible* to the naked eye.

3. *All cards* will be issued from *one Central Office* by 1982, but they will continue to bear separate logos; as Visa and MasterCard for a time.

EFT Report (Electronic Fund Transfer): a publication which goes into most banks printed an article entitled "MASTERCARD," September 17, 1979. It stated:

> "In a speech, John J. Reynolds, President of Interbank Card Association, said that 'the newly named MasterCard will be a full transaction card, rather than just a credit card.'

The report continues, 'In significant ways, Interbank now has brought its EFT strategy in line with Visa's. The debit card will bear the familiar red and ochre logo, in the same way that all Visa cards are blue, white and gold. Even the new magnetic stripe specification adopted for the MasterCard now embraces an element introduced by Visa's *'three-digit service code'* in the discretionary datafield of Track 2. With this code, it will be possible to determine if a card *from one Country* may be used . . . in another Country.' D. Sean Millen, Interbank Senior VP, told EFT Report, 'The real reason it's there is that it would be very difficult to put in later.' "

Please notice that; (1) These new cards *will look like* the old cards, but they are not credit cards, they are transaction cards; and (2) A "3-digit service code" makes them international, which would have to be incorporated later if not in 1980.

An astute banking official divulged to me that the national "3-digit service code" for the United States is "110." My research positively indicates that the "3-digit service code" which will make the card international will be "666."

Information in my file indicates individuals have been issued new cards in 1980 with the prefix "666" embossed on the front. Some of these were Christians who refused to accept the card. Upon returning them to the issuing banks, they were told that another number could be issued them now, but "666" would be on all the cards in 1982! What they were not told, however, was *that in 1982 the number would no longer be embossed on the front,* but, would be encoded on the magnetic tape on the back *invisible to the naked eye.*

It was in August 1980, that I learned J.C. Penney had assigned some regions and billing cycles whose combination resulted in a prefix of "666." See copy of J.C. Penney statement on page 27.

Additionally, it was in August 1980 that Master-Card Service began their switchover from Master-Charge. Likewise, their new MasterCard statements have on them the number "66." See illustration.

‖‖·‖·‖‖·‖‖·‖‖‖·‖·‖‖‖
MARY STEWART RELFE

A "variation" of the Universal Product Code marks is now appearing on MasterCard statements, suggesting the strong possibility that cards of the future may delete the magnetic strip on back and go to the "mark" on cards. See p. 57.

## A Single Card and Number

The Prophet, John, banished to the small island of Patmos some 1900 years ago, was the first to indicate that the last political, economic, and religious systems of this World Age would be operated by an Institution characterized by the number "666," which would cause each individual on the earth to be assigned a number, the NUMERICAL equivalence of "666."

"No man might buy or sell, save he that: (1) had

the *mark;* or (2) the *name* of the beast; or (3) the *NUMBER* of his name."

The wisdom of Verse 18, where the *NUMBER* is mentioned three times, is to understand that the only commerce Christians can conduct during the time of the very end will be by utilizing alternative #3, Verse 17; which is to *know* his number "666," not take his *mark,* "666!"

In 1798, a Methodist Minister, Adam Clarke wrote:

> "The mark of the beast will be an 18 digit number, 6 + 6 + 6." *Adam Clarke Bible Commentary.*

In 1977, Dr. Hanrick Eldeman, Chief Analyst for the European Economic Community, announced that he was ready to begin assigning a number to every person in the world; and that he "plans to use a three six-digital unit, 18 numbers." The Rev. David Webber, in *Point of No Return,* Southwest Radio Church.

It is as difficult for us to conceive of a world without cash as a bank without a vault. Instead of cash, there will be numbers; in lieu of banks there will be computers. Mr. Cantelon indicates in *New Money Or None,* that:

> "For over a decade bankers and technicians of Europe had been feverishly working to establish a new number system."

Meanwhile, bank employees deluged in mountains of cancelled checks were endorsing their noble efforts, and law enforcement agencies were crying, "Away with cash and eliminate crime."

37

In *American Bar Magazine,* a noted Attorney, Mr. Speiser, says:

> "Crime would be virtually eliminated if cash became obsolete. Cash is the only real motive for 90% of the robberies. Hence its liquidation would create miracles in ridding earth's citizens of muggings and holdups."

The advantages of a cashless society are enormous in the eyes of perplexed public officials faced with unprecedented increases in crime. Not only will the absence of cash eliminate robberies, murders, and muggings for money, but equally important will be the elimination of extortion and blackmail. No one would think of extorting a sum of merchandise and having it charged to their card number. Then there is the Black Market contraband led by heroin, opium, LSD, marijuana, and untaxed liquor usually paid for in "cash under the table" deals that would cease to exist. People will have to be discreet with merchandise charged to their personal identification number. To the average person on the streets, this control over buying and selling will appear to be utopia.

The card now ready to be issued, which will have your one number on it will be the result of massive efforts, nationally and internationally.

> "We, the members of the United Nations . . . solemnly proclaim our united determination to work urgently for The Establishment of a New International Economic Order." *U.N. Monthly Chronicle,* May, 1974.

"On May 2, 1976, the United Nations General Assembly declared the establishment of a 'New International Economic Order,' which will include the 'cancellation of all previous debts.' " *Houston Chronicle,* May 5, 1976.

In his article concerning the world's largest computer, February, 1975, Mr. Charles Duncombe of CFN Information Network's Jerusalem Bureau states:

"Dr. Hanrick Eldeman, Chief Analyst of the Common Market Confederacy in Brussels, has revealed that a computerized restoration plan is already under way to straighten out world chaos. A crisis meeting in early 1974 brought together Common Market leaders, advisors and scientists at which time Dr. Eldeman unveiled 'THE BEAST.' It is a gigantic, three story, self-programming computer with the potential of NUMBERING EVERY HUMAN BEING ON EARTH."

Gary Allen in *A Decade Left — Has Orwell's 1984 Come Early?* says:

"Federal planners foresee the day when every citizen will have a *money card* instead of money to spend. The cards would be placed in a machine at each point of purchase, and the charge would be electronically subtracted from the customer's Federal Reserve Account."

In *The Daily Oklahoman,* September 21, 1976, was an article entitled "The Cashless Society Expected to Become Reality Soon.'' It states:

"The long-talked about 'cashless society' is almost here. Bank *debit cards* are expected to go into nationwide use soon."

And the *Progressive Grocer*, November, 1975 says:

"The day will come when *one card* will be good at any terminal, in any store, in any state; said an enthusiastic banking official."

When was this single card and single number projected to become a reality?

"Very soon, many bankers predict, most shoppers will exchange *the wallet full of credit cards they now carry* for a *single, all-purpose* card and number." *Knight News Service*, Miami, Florida.

"The American dollar is under attack again, but, not from Arab oil sheiks or Japanese car manufacturers or inflation or any of the dollar's usual enemies. The dollar is being threatened by, of all things, the computer. Why? Well, picture this: It is 1985 and you are checking out at your neighborhood grocery. By then your food bill might come to something like $99.50. That is irritating, but take heart. You may not have to fumble around with checkbooks or cash. '*Your debit card, please.*' the cashier will say, and you will hand her a thin piece of plastic — *a credit card look-a-like.* Then you will punch in a code number, *your own secret number,* and presto, you've paid for your groceries." *Detroit News,* Gerald L. Nelson, Special Writer.

I was watching ABC's Good Morning America on May 29, 1980, and heard a Federal Reserve Board Official announce the issuance of a new Federal *debit card*:

"A thin piece of plastic which is to be inserted in automatic machines. One must then punch in his own *secret code number* . . . You are not to write your number down, tell it to anyone, or record it anywhere. It must be memorized," the representative stated.

## Problems With the Card

My mind immediately focused on the elderly, the senile, and the mentally retarded, who could neither remember their numbers nor punch them in correctly. Additionally, there is the danger of being murdered or kidnapped for this card. One cannot travel without it. There will always be the possibility of loss or theft of one's card.

"Ye shall not . . . print any marks upon you." Leviticus 19:28.

## Solutions

Almost in a prophetic vein, September 20, 1973, the front cover of *Senior Scholastics,* a secular

41

COVER COPY of SENIOR SCHOLASTIC, September 20, 1973, an excellent secular high school publication depicting the future "buying and selling" system with numbers inserted on the forehead. © 1973 by Scholastic Inc. Reprinted by permission.

42

magazine for high school students, shows a full color artist's rendering of youths from various parts of the world with their numbers tattooed on their foreheads. An article in the issue, "Public Needs and Private Rights — Who Is Watching You?"

> "All buying and selling in the program will be done by computer. No currency, no change, no checks. In the program, people would receive a number that had been assigned them tattooed *in* their wrist or forehead. The number is put on by a laser beam and cannot be felt. The number in the body is not seen with the naked eye and is as permanent as your fingerprints. All items of consumer goods will be marked with a computer mark. The computer outlet in the store which picks up the number on the items at the checkstand will also pick up the number in the person's body and automatically total the price and deduct the amount from the person's 'Special Drawing Rights' account . . ." (See picture.)

Experimentation with non-toxic ink has been conducted using cattle, fish and persons. Some employees of the Pennsylvania Prison System have had a number tattooed on their hands, which when run under the infra-red scanner, programs doors to open for them.

A Washington State University Professor, R. Keith Farrell, invented a laser tattoo gun in 1974 with which he has laser numbered fish in one thirty-billionth of a second. When asked if this gun could be used to number every person in the world, Dr. Farrell replied, "It could indeed be used for such a purpose," reports Rev. David Webber of Southwest Radio Church. (See photograph.)

More recent information has surfaced that the banking industry in conjunction with the United States Government has completed testing of a soft injectable plastic manufactured by a laboratory in Orlando, Florida. Upon a subcutaneous injection of the liquid substance, it smooths out under the skin much like water does on a flat surface; becomes semi-hard, forming a permanent under-skin shield on which the tattoo gun imprints the person's number. Further information indicates that banks are now ready to begin imprinting these permanent numbers "*in* the right hand or *in* the forehead." Revelation 13:16. Note that John said "*IN*" not "*ON!*"

## Beast of Brussels or Luxembourg

Brussels, Belgium, headquarters of the European Economy is the location of the Main Switching Center in the International Computer hook-up developed by Burroughs Corporation that will accomodate the transfer of electronic funds internationally. This Control Center occupies three floors of the headquarter's thirteen story building. It is here Dr. Hanrick Eldeman, Chief Computer Analyst, is currently directing efforts to assign every person on earth an 18-digit NUMBER.

44

Dr. R. Keith Farrell laser tattooed these fish in one thirty-billionth of a second. Photo courtesy of Southwest Radio Church, Oklahoma City.

An article appeared in the *San Jose Mercury,* August 8, 1975, entitled "How About This?"

"The Beast is described as being a gigantic computer occupying three floors of the administration building of the Common Market's headquarters. It indicates that computer scientists are working on a master plan to assign numbers to each individual on earth. This number could be used for trading purposes — buying and selling. The reporters suggest that a 'digital number' could be 'laser-tattooed' on the forehead or back of the hand. This 'inter-

The European Economic Community's 3-story computer complex in Luxembourg. The largest in the world, it is called "The Beast." Photo courtesy of Southwest Radio Church, Oklahoma City.

national mark' could do away with all currency. 'No member could buy or sell without having an assignment of a digital mark,' " the article states. *New Money or None,* Willard Cantelon.

Dr. Emil Gaverluk: "Can you tell us something about the big computer in Brussels which has been called 'the Beast'?"

Dr. Patrick Fisher: "It has been in existence for four years or so. Through use of credit cards, it has been easy to put almost all the trading nations into the memory banks. *You and I are tied into this computer* by one or more keys: our social security number, our driver's license, our birth certificate, our passport number, and whatever credit cards we use. Every move you have made, and every penny that you have paid to Internal Revenue each year is all on record. The computer capacity was set for 2 billion people four years ago. Basically these were from the industrial trading nations: those people who are traveling, those people who are using credit cards, those people who are using international borders to come in and out of a country that they visit."

Dr. Gaverluk: "Let me stress that again — *every individual who is a member of one of these industrial nations is already in that computer?*"

Dr. Fisher: "*Yes, he is.* And every move he's made, any change of address, what jobs, what his earning capacity has been, and what he has paid to the Internal Revenue at the end of each year —"

47

Dr. Gaverluk: "I don't think most people realize that."

The above is an excerpt of interview of Dr. Emil Gaverluk, Scientist and Minister, Southwest Radio Church with Dr. Patrick Fisher, renowned Canadian Computer Scientist.

Additionally, we have learned in 1980 that the little "Beast of Brussels" is giving way to the real Beast of Luxembourg, the most gigantic Computer Complex in the world, due for completion in late 1980. It is located in Luxembourg in the Monet Building.

## SWIFT

In the mid 1970's Nancy French, writing in *Computer World* states that:

> "SWIFT (SOCIETY FOR WORLDWIDE IN-TERBANK FINANCIAL TRANSAC-TIONS) is establishing a worldwide communications network linking 240 members worldwide. This system is so designed that ANY type of computer system in the world can *become a participant.*
>
> "Burroughs Corporation has been selected by the Society for Worldwide Inter-bank Financial Telecommunications (SWIFT) to supply data processing and data communications equipment which will be used in a NEW INTERNATIONAL TELECOM-MUNICATIONS NETWORK, SWIFT, which is based in Brussels, and currently has a membership of 246 banks with a private com-

48

munications system for the transmission of payment and other messages associated with international banking. Initially, the SWIFT network will be comprised of switching centers in *Brussels* and Amsterdam . . . such centers will be linked to Burroughs' data concentrators, initially in Amsterdam, Brussels, Copenhagen, Frankfurt, Helsinki, London, Milan, Montreal, New York, Oslo, Paris, Stockholm, Vienna and Zurich. The data concentrators in each country will be connected to terminals in *member banks* in that country. Most messages transmitted on the SWIFT network will be delivered anywhere in the system within a minute of being entered." *Burroughs Clearing House,* January, 1975.

Quoting from *The Capital Voice,* Washington, D.C.:

"This SWIFT bank is being built (not by accident) close by the Federal Reserve Field Office, a most strategic and most sensitive spot. Actually it is to be the Washington, D.C., headquarters for international banking transactions, but controlled in Brussels. Surrounded by an aura of mystery, and a topic of much discussion, this operation is known by the bankers associated with the European Common Market, some of whom are now moving into Culpeper without fanfare. By the use of signs, symbols, numbers, and mystical figures processed through a sophisticated computer

49

system supported by electronic devices that stagger the imagination, these top financiers have acquired the technology along with the business acumen which enables them to control the structure and the manipulation of the world's currency. It is called, 'SWIFT.' Its membership consists of hundreds of the most important banks in Western Europe, the United States, Canada and Japan. Now this fabulous telecommunications system is reaching right into Culpeper, only a stone's throw from the offices of *The Capital Voice*. But the building (under construction, and ready for occupancy next year) is designed to resemble a warehouse rather than a business block. It is costing, along with this elaborate electronic equipment, some $15 million. Experts, mostly from Europe, are among the administrators of the Culpeper operation. It is doubtful if any of these men are aware that institution of the SWIFT bank is in the fulfillment of Bible prophecy. These are men of integrity and high motivation. But, THIS IS THE SYSTEM THAT ANTICHRIST WILL SEIZE AT THE PROPHETIC MOMENT. It will control the common currency of the world (now in formation). It is the system under which, according to Revelation 13, that 'No man might buy or sell, save he that had the mark, or the name of the beast, or the number of his name.' So, the international bankers have already prepared the way for the

Antichrist . . ."

## Electronic Fund Transfer

Let us now focus on how near we are in 1981, to the Electronic Money System being locally functional in the United States. When shall we be able to use a single card in a retail store and transact all our business; pay our utility bills, transfer funds from one account to another, make deposits and withdrawals, and even apply for a mortgage? The System is already here! The equipment to facilitate these transactions is in our department stores even here in Montgomery, Alabama. Gayfer's, for example, is already equipped with the POS Terminals; Electronic (Cashless) Registers.

Let us now focus on a big bank in the United States which is pioneering this system. ELECTRONIC MONEY. *Chase Manhattan Bank and Electronic Money. EFT Report* (305 E. 56th Street, New York, New York 10022).

> "A sophisticated point-of-sale system is quietly operated by the Chase Manhattan Bank. *In one of the banking industry's best-kept secrets,* Chase now has Interfaces to the computer systems of 13 different retailers. The bank thus is indirectly linked to hundreds of electronic cash registers (or POS terminals) in department and specialty stores." "These stores are located from New England, to the Southeast, to the Midwest." Phillip J. Riese, the Vice-President in charge of this program

says, 'We see ourselves assisting merchants nationwide in performing non-cash transactions.' By offering this system to merchants on a nationwide basis, a network will be created that will allow The Chase Manhattan Bank at a later time, to have a national 'EFTS' presence. *It is highly possible that banking in the future will take place at the point of sale.* It seems to us [EFT Report says] that Chase *already* is engaged in national EFT to a certain extent. Branch banking is becoming more and more expensive, observes Paul G. Tongue, a Senior VP, 'while electronic banking is becoming less and less expensive.' "

With the full implementation of the POS Terminals in all retail outlets, expect to see a drastic decrease in the need for branch banks, and subsequent mass closings. Each POS Terminal in every retail store will be equivalent to a branch bank at a fraction of the cost.

## Electronic Age of "Six"

IBM has an extensive numerical coding system. All IBM products in the Sixties were prefixed with the digit ''2.'' In the Seventies, IBM computer devices were assigned the prefix ''3.'' Likewise, international credit cards which were prefixed with ''2'' in the Sixties advanced to the prefixes ''3,'' ''4,'' and ''5'' in the Seventies.

Presently, the computers systems have reached such a level of sophistication that another digit is required, one which can be programmed both in its normal position and inverted. The perfect digit is "6"; inverted it is still a usable number, "9."

At this moment the entire world is being linked up for the issuance of the new International Card by which each individual's funds can be electronically transferred. This card is due to be issued during the year 1982. The initial digit on this card (which is now ready to be issued) will be advanced to the digit "6." No other digit could have so conveniently accommodated this massive system. As early as 1978 a friend of mine was assigned her own personal indentification Number, "6110." She did not know that it was a preview of the new "international prefix 6," and the United States Code "110."

IBM and NCR are leaders in the manufacture of Point of Sale Systems, which we still prefer to call "Cash Registers." The National Cash Register, Model 304, a popular supermarket system, now works on a series of 6 cores. (A core is a ferromagnetic loop with two states of polarization, allowing for changing directions of current to perform switching functions.) The 6 cores work in conjunction with 60 displacements X 6 — one character, or one bit of information. The formula for this system is simply: 6 60 6. In order to number an item (or a person's card) the transaction must be prefixed "six hundred, threescore, and six"!

## Social Security Number, Please?

As the Card System is being narrowed down to one card and one number, we can expect a rapid phase-out of all old numbers; gas card numbers, passport numbers, birth certificate numbers, and driver license numbers. Research done in the summer of 1980 indicates that:

1. Most numbers have already been abandoned in favor of the Social Security number.

2. The Social Security number is already tied to all bank accounts, checking and savings.

3. The Social Security number is required by the Internal Revenue Service on all tax-paying/reporting transactions.

4. Some states have cancelled driver license numbers and substituted the state wide use of Social Security numbers on driver licenses, Oklahoma, for example.

5. Medicaid, Medicare, and Blue Cross have begun using the Social Security numbers.

6. My most recent Certified Flight Instructor Certificate has my Social Security number on it.

7. My Civil Air Patrol identification number is my Social Security.

8. The new Telco credit card application from South Central Bell uses the prefix ''666'' followed by the applicant's Social Security number.

### The Worldwide Money Card Number

I am therefore conjecturing that the next international card will utilize the $6 + 6 + 6$ digits projected by the Rev. Clarke in 1798; which is aligned with Dr. Eldeman's announcement in 1977, of 3 six-digital units; an 18-digit number.

I expect the code sequencing to be thusly:

- 666 — the International Code which will activate the World Computer.

- 110 — the National Code which will activate the Central United States computer.

- 205 — or, your area telephone code, indicating your locality.

- Your nine digit Social Security Number.

This construction will make my own personal number to be:

$$\frac{666\ 110}{6} + \frac{205\ 419}{6} + \frac{386\ 968}{6}$$

Three six-digit units!

Expect some changes to be forthcoming since a few Social Security numbers are identical. Fingerprints on cards will solve identification problems. In the October 1980 issue of *Next* magazine, Harold Green, President of Comparator Systems says: ''Your future identification card may contain only the unique whorls of one index finger.''

I cannot be totally dogmatic about this sequence. I honestly confess that this is not a Divine Revelation. It is most assuredly a prudent assessment resulting from over twenty-five years and thousands of hours of Bible study and in-depth research on Bible Prophecies as they relate to current events. Yet, I humbly confess

that "We see through a glass darkly," but, *we do see!*
Bible research is truly "Precept upon precept, line
upon line, here a little, there a little." Isaiah 28:10.

## The Mark Is Designed for 1984

"And he causeth all . . . to receive a mark . . ."
In Greek this word mark is charagma, which literally
denotes a stamp, an impress, and is translated mark.
Notice that John did not say that he causeth all to
receive a number in the right hand or forehead. This
astute prophet could have certainly delineated between
a series of numbers, and an unexplained stamp or mark.

The new Electronic Eyes being installed on these
computer cash registers do not understand numbers,
they only read marks which they translate into mean-
ingful digits. The Laser Scanners do not know what to
do with a $1.39 price on a tube of toothpaste which was
not put there for their eyes, but for ours. These Electronic Eyes scan the product until they find the Universal Product Code, a one inch square of vertical lines of
varying lengths, widths, and separations of lines which
provide encoded information that programs the Computer to: (1) Compute the sales price of the item, (2) Take
the item out of inventory, (3) Place the item on a new
order blank, and (4) Total the price of all items scanned.

Additionally, these Computers are equipped to
receive our personal identification numbers (from our
International Money Cards), and, when punched in,
instantly debits our accounts and credits the store account at the bank. *These systems are designed to go a
together.* The same Electronic Eye which scans the
will in the near future scan the marks that

will be required to be inserted on the body. This will eliminate the necessity of the clerk's additional step of punching in our numbers from the Card.

Transitioning the world from the Card to the insertion of the encoded marks on the body will be made simple according to an article in *Navy Times,* August 4, 1980. ". . . New computerized identification cards have been approved by the Defense Department that will be introduced in 1981, and money for them has been budgeted for fiscal 1982 . . . They will be hooked into a worldwide computer system. The official said that, although most plans include a card with a magnetic stripe, one possible contractor *would use optical stripes (marks) such as those used in the Universal Product Code seen on grocery packages . . . .*" This entire Electronic Funds Transfer System is a "means of massive surveillance of the population," warned Art Bushkin, official of the Commerce Department, *who added, "by 1984 the system will be common." Chicago Tribune,* August 2, 1979, page 8. Oh, what a small task of transferring the encoded mark from the Card to the body!

### The Head/Hand Scan Machine Is Ready!

"The 'Hand Scan' Machine is now a living reality," so stated an astute banking official, Lowell R. Brisben, May 31, 1980, on one of America's leading independent television stations. He added that this machine eliminates the need for cards, but identifies the person's "secret number," as it electronically scans the right hand. Christian Cable Communication is to be commended for its involvement and assistance in the initial release of this information.

A strong hint as to the time of implementation of

this system has made George Orwell's 1984 unbelievably accurate. Quoting from *The Cronkhites,* Polson, Montana, "The Internal Revenue Service refund office has printed a trial run of their checks for 1984 and twenty-five accidentally got mailed recently in California." On the back of the checks are these instructions: "Do not cash this check unless the recipient has a number on either his right hand or on his forehead."

In addition, in July and August, 1980, the Internal Revenue Service mailed scores of Social Security checks to recipients with instructions for cashing them on the back being: *"The proper identification Mark in the right hand or forehead."* Upon the banks' refusal to cash these checks amidst much confusion and denials, the IRS admitted their mistake thusly: "THESE GOVERNMENT CHECKS REQUIRING A MARK IN A PERSON'S RIGHT HAND OR FOREHEAD ARE NOT TO BE PUT INTO USE UNTIL 1984." *The Scroll,* August, 1980, by Evangelist Darrell Dunn.

While some specifics remain vague, of this we are certain: All commerce will be conducted in the near future with a number, a name, or an identifying mark in the hand or forehead. It is my sincere deduction that the "mark of the beast" will not be the insertion of numbers per se on the body, but of vertical lines which will represent encoded messages and digits. These appeared on the foreheads and hands of persons 1900 years ago to the Prophet John as "stamps, or impresses; marks."

Right on John, right on!

And, George Orwell, you were a diviner!

# In Summation

I unreservedly view the international usage of the number "666" by the present World System, to be presided over soon by Mr. 666, the False Messiah, as the Third Most Significant Fulfillment of Bible Prophecy in the Church Age (the past 2000 years).

When the astounding and irrefutable truth of the present usage of the number "666" throughout the economies of the world, and more particularly our credit (?) cards, is disseminated to the public via publication of this and other material, Christendom will explode with outrage. The storm of protests will run the gamut from one end of the pendulum to the other. There will be those with good intentions who will herald the card as the sin of the mark of the Beast. Additionally, there will be those representing the other extreme, with good intentions, who will argue that the card will just be a more convenient way of transacting business as checks were more convenient than cash.

In the center of every great storm there is an eye. There will also be those center-thrust Christians whose response to these truths will drive them to switch off the television and began to study the Bible in one hand and a newspaper in the other. These will not be "destroyed for lack of knowledge."

Present day Christianity owes a debt of gratitude to the emminent Doctors Patrick Fisher and Emil Gaverluk, who early in 1979 correctly sequenced the issuance of this new card as the last step before the requirement by the World Dictator to receive this number in some form in one's forehead or hand.

From this and other information we have been able to deduct that:

1. The number on this card will most assuredly be the same number as that which subsequently will be encoded, and required to be inserted on one's body.

2. The person who accepts and uses this one card and number will surely become more firmly enmeshed in this One World System. (When my friend and colleague, Sally O'Brien received her J.C. Penney statement for August, 1980, no one had consulted with her or notified her that the number on her old card was obsolete, nor have they yet issued a new card. Her statement, however, reflected her account number was changed from 516-747-847-7-2, to 666-742-522-42. Further examination of her 1978 Sears credit card, revealed that it incorporated this code into a suffix ''666.'' See illustration. I facetiously said, ''Sally, you are already a part of the Antichrist's system.'' She quickly responded, ''As soon as I get back to California, I am going to draw out of my savings, pay this account off, and get out of the System.''

3. If you are a Christian, you should pay off your debts! Do not owe your soul to the Antichrist, as the Egyptians owed theirs to the Pharoah. Genesis 47:15-25. You will be here when the Antichrist shall be revealed! II Thessalonians 2:1-3.

4. While there are many things we can do to reduce our involvement with this System, it is highly doubtful that Christians can live totally independent of it. It appears that Christians can use alternative #3, as indeed they are already; but we cannot take the mark. See update in appendix.

"If any man worship the beast and his image, and receive his mark in his forehead, or in his hand, the same shall *drink* of the wine of the wrath of God . . ." Revelation 14:9-10.

Ladies and gentlemen, I have a relentless urgency to share with you that this world is now standing on the threshold of the most critical decade in the history of mankind. I had for years charted the end of this World Order as closely corresponding to the close of this century. Today, I am not at all certain that one person reading these lines will see 1990 before they see His Eternal Majesty, King Wonderful, Jesus Christ, Son of the Living God, "revealed from heaven in flaming fire taking vengeance on them that know not God and obey not the Gospel." II Thessalonians 1:8.

Without qualification, I unequivocally assert that this is the most somber moment ever thrust upon Christians! It is reminiscent of another moment of grave sobriety in the history of the Church. I was a teenager at that time, but well apprised of its prophetic significance by my mother, a Bible scholar. We listened (with the world) to the voting progress in the United Nations. Finally, the last nation cast its deciding vote, and a name was given to a little middle eastern nation. It would be Israel not Zion, by one vote.

My mother gathered us around her and announced, "Children, what took place this day, May 14, 1948, is the most significant event since Jesus Christ was born 2000 years ago. Until Israel became a nation again, Jesus Christ could not come back to the earth. From this time on we can 'look up, and lift up our heads for our redemption draweth nigh.' "

In my teenage mind I believed that He was coming back that day . . . then the next day . . . and the next. The somber note of the imminence of Christ's return filtered to the nucleus of every cell of my being with such force that I could not pry myself from its grasp, and admittedly have been a servant of this truth for the past 32 years.

If I could, like my mother, gather you readers around me I would say:

> "The sobriety which I felt when that dramatic fulfillment of prophecy occurred and Israel became a nation is totally and greatly eclipsed by the more dramatic fulfillment of the prophecy of John who proclaimed 1900 years ago, that the last seven years of this age would be lived under a One World System of buying and selling characterized by a heretofore unknown numerical entity, '666.' This System is with us; and the 'Man,' the numerical value of whose name will also be '666' is about to be revealed. When he is, the countdown for this World Order will be 'T Minus 7 Years And Counting!' "

62

Ah, Bill Gaither, you were in the Spirit when you declared:

*". . . Regal robes are now unfolded;*
*Heaven's grandstand's all in place;*
*Heaven's choir is now assembled*
*. . . To sing 'Amazing Grace.'*
*Yes, the King is coming, the King is coming,*
*Praise God, He's coming for me!"*

*This book is published by:*
Ministries, Inc.
Post Office Box 4038
Montgomery, Alabama 36104 (205) 262-4891

# CHAPTER III

*"Perilous times . . ."*
*"When these things begin to come*
*to pass . . ."*

II TIMOTHY 3:1, LUKE 21:28.

# THE "666" SYSTEM

## (The One World Government)

It was a brisk November Sabbath Friday evening that I stood at the Wailing Wall, the only remains of the old Jewish Temple, shivering equally from the wind blown rain and the unabating sounds of the prayers of the Jewish faithful. Pathos erupted within me when I was told that most of the prayers were for the coming of the Messiah and the ". . . rebuilding of thy Temple, O God."

I lamented that the blindness that had happened to Israel 2000 years ago would not be lifted until they accepted a False Messiah who would subsequently desecrate their next temple and rule the nations of the world as no tyrant in all of history. What further saddened me was that this Dictator will be the consummation of the hopes and dreams of all mankind, and his brief seven year regime will become the world's greatest nightmare. He will make Nero and Hitler look like gentlemen as he exercises his unprecedented endowment of power over all nations of the earth.

"And all that dwell upon the earth *shall* worship him . . . whose names are not written in the book of life." Revelation 13:8.

## Political Aspects

The end of this world order will be characterized by upheavals (plural; "perilous *times,*" "these *things*") that will result in an apparent need for this One World Government. Each upheaval, whether political, economic, social or religious, will be a phenomenon in itself. The identifying clue will be that all of these will be occurring simultaneously. These end-time upheavals will not be isolated to one or a few nations; as historically, nations have experienced wars, inflations, economic morass, and political collapse; but *never have all nations experienced all these upheavals* concurrently! Buried in such local, national, and international chaos, leaders will recognize and acquiesce to the one ray of hope that emerges, the as yet untried and highly touted One World Government.

## Historical Aspects

Nebuchadnezzar, an absolute monarch, was one of history's first aspirants for this lofty position, and indeed his reign most typified the reign of the Antichrist. Everyone was ordered to worship his "image" (60 cubits high, 6 cubits wide, 6 instruments used); a type of worship the Antichrist will also require. Both systems of worship conspicuously bear the number "666."

A cold March day found me trudging along up the Acropolis in Athens against a 40-knot wind, struggling to hear the guide narrate the exploits of Alexander The Great with whom he was quite enamored.

Alexander's expressed dream was:

> "to found a world state in which all men would be brothers. To encourage the fusion of his Asiatic and European subjects, he had eighty of his officers take Asiatic wives . . . he took a second wife Barsine, daughter of Darius III. Alexander thought of mankind as citizens of *One Great Community,* the world. He gave the entire realm a uniform coinage, and Greek became the international language for both government and commerce." *Compton's Encyclopedia.*

Some while later, I was being shown the place in the Colosseum in Rome, where many Christians were fed to lions. I remembered how the Caesars demanded homage from the inhabitants of the empire, but in addition, worship as a god also. Runners were sent to the far flung reaches of the Roman Empire requiring subjects to affix their signatures to affidavits acquiescing to worship of the Emperor, another type of the Antichrist to come. (The name Nero Caesar numerically equals the sum of 666.) A special day was set aside each year, Augustean Day, for this purpose. Never, however, did a Caesar demand to be worshipped as the God of Gods which would have been blasphemy to their polytheistic system of Roman Mythology (many gods). Conversely, Antichrist, the False Messiah, will be monotheistic; finally "exhalting himself above all that is called God." II Thessalonians 2:4.

Blown-up view of "all seeing eye of a deity, the pyramid, and the Latin words, Novus Ordo Seclorum," as it was designed for the U.S. one dollar bill. It means the New World Order which is the "666 System."

Modern efforts took on new impetus in 1776 when the United States one dollar bill was designed with the all seeing eye of a deity over a pyramid beneath which are the words in Latin "Novus Ordo Seclorum," which literally means "a new world order." The world is witnessing the formation of this New Order and most of us living today will see it fully implemented. The common medium of exchange will be numbers operated by computers.

In 1838, Mr. Rothschild said, "Let me issue and control a nation's money, and I care not who writes its laws." This family has been joined by a few other "international bankers" who have made their business lending money to governments, placing governments in debt to an unseen, but powerful few.

In *Tragedy and Hope,* Dr. Carrol Quigley, admits:

> "there does exist . . . an international network whose aim is to create a world system of financial control in private hands able to dominate the political system of each country and the economy of the world. The individual's freedom and choice will be controlled within very narrow alternatives by the fact that *he will be numbered from birth* and followed as a number until his death."

## Contemporary Aspects

As a child, I listened as my father analyzed and rejected as unsound the One Worldism espoused by President Roosevelt. Then came the news of the first detonation of an atomic bomb August 6, 1945, on Hiroshima. A flood of voices was raised on the behalf of a One World Government for human survival. One particular voice was heard above the crowd, Albert

Einstein . . .

"The secret of the bomb should be committed to a World Government and the USA should announce its readiness to give it to a World Government."

The Preamble of the United Nations Charter reads:

"We the people of the United Nations *determined to save succeeding generations from the scourge of war . . .*"

The United Nations has become the agency coordinating this World Wide Federated State.

"At the end of the 1970's, *the World Body* (United Nations) had 150 member states." *Reader's Digest Wideworld Atlas, 1979.*

The Almanac table of nations indicated in 1978 that there were only 152 recognized nations in the world.

I have copies of two treaties in my study that leave no doubt that the United States is cooperating with the United Nations in this effort. President Carter signed these two treaties at the United Nations, October 5, 1978, which cancels the right of Americans to own private property. If ratified by two-thirds of the Senate, these will give the United Nations the right to abolish private property, as the United States Constitution states that treaties are the highest law in the land. The names of the two treaties are:

United Nations Covenant on Civil and Political

Rights.

United Nations Covenant on Economic, Social and Cultural rights.

Upon reading these treaties, my brother, Bernard Stewart, wrote both Alabama Senator Helflin, and Congressman Dickinson. Their replies are shown.

In his book, *Politics Among Nations,* Hans J. Morgenthau wrote:

> "There is no shirking the conclusion that international peace cannot be permanent without a World State . . . and in no period of modern history was civilization more in need of permanent peace, and hence of a world state."

Dr. Saul H. Mendlovitch wrote recently:

> "There is no longer a question of whether or not there will be a world government. There is a continuing drive to dilute, then dissolve the sovereignty of the United States of America for the new World Order, a new international economic order."

There have been for years at least sixteen World Agencies working on behalf of its formation. Dr. Jack Van Impe, Box J, Royal Oak, Michigan 48068, gives a broader coverage of this in his booklet, *Your Startling Future.*

1. *WORLD BANK* (International Bank for Reconstruction and Development). It was designed to internationalize money standards and to place all the money power of the world in the hands of one agency.

WILLIAM L. DICKINSON
2ND DISTRICT, ALABAMA

WASHINGTON OFFICE:
2465 RAYBURN HOUSE OFFICE BUILDING
PHONE: AREA CODE (202) 225-2901
WASHINGTON, D.C. 20515

2ND DISTRICT COUNTIES:
BARBOUR      CRENSHAW
BULLOCK      DALE
BUTLER       GENEVA
COFFEE       HENRY
CONECUH      HOUSTON
COVINGTON    MONTGOMERY
             PIKE

# Congress of the United States
## House of Representatives
### Washington, D.C. 20515

WALTER J. BAMBERG
FIELD REPRESENTATIVE

DISTRICT OFFICES:
ROOM 301 FEDERAL COURT BUILDING
15 LEE STREET
PHONE: AREA CODE (205) 832-7292
MONTGOMERY, ALABAMA 36104

FEDERAL BUILDING
100 WEST TROY STREET
PHONE: AREA CODE (205) 794-8680
DOTHAN, ALABAMA 36303

COMMITTEES:
ARMED SERVICES
HOUSE ADMINISTRATION
JOINT COMMITTEE ON PRINTING

August 18, 1980

Mr. Bernard Stewart
6611 South Monticello Drive
Montgomery, Alabama 36117

Dear Mr. Stewart:

Thank you very much for your recent letter which discussed the U.N. Covenant on Civil and Political Rights and the U.N. Covenant on Economic Social and Cultural Rights.

I appreciate hearing from you about this matter. I have been advised by the Senate Foreign Relations Committee, which has jurisdiction over treaties, that these treaties have not been ratified and are still pending before the Committee awaiting action. Because the Senate has exclusive jurisdiction over treaties, there is little I can do in this area. I will, however, monitor all action taken in this area and will also share your concern with members of the Foreign Relations Committee.

I might also suggest that you contact members of that Committee to express your concern. I have enclosed a listing of the members for your information.

Again, thank you for taking the time to write me about this important matter. If I can be of further assistance to you in the future, please do not hesitate to let me know. In the meantime, my kindest regards.

Sincerely yours,

Bill

WM. L. DICKINSON

**FOREIGN RELATIONS**
DSOB-4229 .................... 44651

Frank Church, of Idaho, Chairman.
Claiborne Pell, of Rhode Island.
George McGovern, of South Dakota.
Joseph R. Biden, Jr., of Delaware.
John Glenn, of Ohio.
Richard (Dick) Stone, of Florida.
Paul S. Sarbanes, of Maryland.
~~Edmund S. Muskie, of Maine~~
Edward Zorinsky, of Nebraska.
Paul Tsongas, of Massachusetts

Jacob K. Javits, of New York.
Charles H. Percy, of Illinois.
Howard H. Baker, Jr., of Tennessee.
Jesse Helms, of North Carolina.
S. I. (Sam) Hayakawa, of California.
Richard G. Lugar, of Indiana.

address: United States Senate
Washington, D.C. 10510

71

EDWARD M. KENNEDY, MASS., CHAIRMAN

BIRCH BAYH, IND.                      STROM THURMOND, S.C.
ROBERT C. BYRD, W. VA.                CHARLES MC C. MATHIAS, JR., MD.
JOSEPH R. BIDEN, JR., DEL.            PAUL LAXALT, NEV.
JOHN C. CULVER, IOWA                  ORRIN G. HATCH, UTAH
HOWARD M. METZENBAUM, OHIO            ROBERT DOLE, KANS.
DENNIS DE CONCINI, ARIZ.             THAD COCHRAN, MISS.
PATRICK J. LEAHY, VT.                 ALAN K. SIMPSON, WYO.
MAX BAUCUS, MONT.
HOWELL HEFLIN, ALA.

STEPHEN BREYER, CHIEF COUNSEL

# United States Senate

COMMITTEE ON THE JUDICIARY

WASHINGTON, D.C. 20510

August 21, 1980

Mr. Bernard Stewart
6111 South Monticello Drive
Montgomery, AL  36117

Dear Bernard:

Thank you for your recent communication requesting certain information about two treaties:  International Covenant on Economic, Social and Cultural Rights and International Covenant on Civil and Political Rights.

These two treaties were adopted by the United Nations General Assembly in 1966 and entered into force for the countries which ratified or acceded to them in 1976.

The basis for your assertion relative to property rights is found in the fact that the Covenants were intended to put into binding treaty form the rights set forth in the 1948 Universal Declaration of Human Rights, adopted by the United Nations General Assembly as an Assembly resolution.  The Declaration in Article 17 states:

1.  Everyone has the right to own property alone as well as in association with others.

2.  No one shall be arbitrarily deprived of his property.

However, this language is not found in either of the Covenants. The omission of this language from the Covenants, it is argued, means that these documents nullify the rights set forth in the Declaration, Article 17.

The Covenants, as treaties, will have to be approved by the Senate before the United States can ratify them and thus become bound by them.  They were submitted to the Senate by the President on February 23, 1978.  It has been recommended that the Senate include in its resolution of ratification a declaration of understanding on behalf of the United States that nothing in the Covenants nullify the rights set forth in Article 17 of the Declaration.

2. *WORLD FOOD ORGANIZATION* (established to standardize levels of nutrition throughout the world . . . to more equitably distribute the food of the world). When this conference last convened in Rome, it was loudly calling attention to this inequity when citing the fact that 57 million people starved to death in the world in 1979.

". . . In January 1977 there were four billion people in the world, of whom two-thirds (or 2.7 billion) lived in countries with median incomes below $300 a head, while one-third lived in countries with median incomes above $3,000 per head." John Hackett, *The Third World War.*

*The secular person would call this inequity. The Christian knows this is the "God Factor."* Jacob I loved, Esau I hated . . . I will have mercy on whom I will have mercy."

3. *WORLD HEALTH ORGANIZATION;* established to internationalize medicine, surgery, and treatments of all diseases. Dr. Jack Van Impe indicates, "This will be the instrument used to commit political opponents to mental institutions thousands of miles from home."

4. *INTERNATIONAL LABOR ORGANIZATION;* established to standardize labor standards throughout the world. Dr. Van Impe says, "This will be the vehicle for the dissemination of Socialism and promotion of the One World Philosophy."

5. *INTERNATIONAL MONETARY FUND:* established to promote international trade and standard-

ize commerce and industry. This will make it very simple for the Antichrist to issue his decree that no man might buy or sell except he receive the mark of the beast.

And eleven others including, (1) *International Trade Organization,* (2) *World Meteriologist Association,* (3) *Universal Postal Union,* (4) *International Civil Aviation Organization,* etc.

And finally, ABC's Harry Reasoner made his voice heard June 18, 1974. ''The only eventual answer is some kind of World government . . . whether it is Capitalist or Communist.''

Since we are so near the ultimate implementation of this One World Government, when and where did it officially begin? The Treaty of Rome in 1957 was the precursor. The magazine of the European Common Market acquiesces to their fulfilling Bible prophecy relative to the end of the age revival of the Roman Empire. European Community states:

''The EEC (European Economic Community) Rome Treaty supports the interpretations of the books of Ezekiel, Daniel, and Revelation that this 'last days' kingdom is a new Roman Empire.''

However, the legality of the One World Government waited for Holland.

### Dutch Motion for One World

''A new move towards a One World Government was recently initiated by Holland. The motion, introduced by a Socialist deputy in the Netherlands Assembly was passed on to the Common Market Commission in Brussels where it received approval of the Commission. The Dutch motion called for European elections; 355 members would be elected to a Federal European Parliament which, if all goes as planned, will unite Western Europe under a single Socialist Government . . . The term of office would be five years and a Socialist-Communist majority would be inevitable.'' *The Review of the News,* December 3, 1975.

The first European election was held in 1979, which set up 410 members of the first European Parliament in over a thousand years. The beautiful Palace of Europe has just been completed in Strasbourg, France, to provide facilities for the Parliamentary Sessions. It has convened twice already.

Greece became the tenth member of the EEC when the Accession Treaty was signed May 28, 1979. It became the tenth member January 1, 1981. Thus, the ten toe (ten Horn) federation seen by Daniel about 500 B.C. has emerged as: Italy, France, Germany, Belgium, Netherlands, Luxembourg, Ireland, Britain, Denmark, and Greece. Other nations may merge into this alliance from which the World Dictator, the False Messiah, will herald.

The United States efforts have become more bold within the past few years.

''Carter is concerned now about organizing what he calls a 'world structure of peace.' He has urged the Chinese to come out of isolation and take a part in creating a new world political order. Carter's foreign policy, promoting a 'World Government,' is not a new concept, but until the advent of Henry Kissinger's influence on our Presidents it was cloaked with secrecy. As Kissinger became prominent in the last two Administrations the 'One World Government' concept became open policy.'' *Fort Lauderdale News,* July 25, 1978.

Paul Scott of the *Washington News,* December 1974, reported:

''Whether he fully realizes it or not, President Ford has put his stamp of approval on Secretary of State Henry Kissinger's grand design foreign policy of the establishment of a loosely knitted World Government before the end of the 1970's. By calling for the development of a global strategy and policy for food and oil within the frame work of the United Nations, the President clearly signaled his acceptance of the 'New International Order' being sought by Kissinger.''

''A meeting was held May 24, 1976, through July 4, 1976, in Valley Forge Park, King of Prussia, Pennsylvania to formulate a new WORLD CONSTITUTION, elaborating a Bill of Human Rights for the world and setting up a permanent Secretariat of Humanists there to superintend the Government of the World . . .'' as reported by the *Borger New*

## Deception Deployed

I observe in our relentless and inevitable march toward this One World Government the most subtle ways devised by man to launch its acceptance upon us.

A famous painting of Hogarth comes to mind of a man in a cell, seated on a heap of straw, chained like a wild beast to the wall; yet he smiles, laughs and sings. He thinks that he is the Monarch of a great empire. The cell is his palace, the heap of moulded straw in his throne. His rags are his coronation robe; the keepers of the prison who peer in through the graded windows are his soldiers. He is a lunatic. Of all the thoughts that surface as one studies the painting is, ''Oh how deceived he is.'' Could you believe me if I told you that the United States generally, and Christians particularly, are as deceived as Hogarth's lunatic?

## Methods

In magazines, newspapers, reporting, entertainment, advertising, and music this One Worldism is presented in stately fashion. For example, in *Business Week,* March 24, 1980, I discovered many full page *advertisements* promoting the concept; for example:

1. ''One of the largest banks in the *WORLD* is taking a new path to INTERCEPT the future . . . We have replaced the account officer with a relationship manager. As the name implies, he or she has WORLDWIDE responsibility. The entire resources

of our *World Class* Bank. BANKERS TRUST COMPANY (Worldwide).

2. When you want a *World Class* Bank to give you World Class Loans . . . BANK OF MONTREAL.

3. ARA, because the *WORLD* will never outgrow its need for service.

4. MANUFACTURERS HANOVER, the financial source *Worldwide,* etc. etc . . . I highly recommend the magazine.

I am looking at this moment at an astounding Publication, HEW (SSA) 78-10171, a Marriage Annoucement of our Social Security system with that of Western Europe! This booklet is entitled *"INTER-NATIONAL AGREEMENT On Social Security, Between The UNITED STATES and ITALY"!*

In some of those far away places with strange sounding names, I have listened to:

*"I'd like to build the* **WORLD** *a home,*
*And furnish it with love,*
*Grow apple trees and honey bees*
*And snow white turtle doves.*
*I'd like to teach the* **WORLD** *to sing*
*In perfect harmony,*
*I'd like to hold it in my arms*
*And keep it company."*

And there is;

*"What the* **WORLD** *needs now is love, sweet love."*

**International agreement on social security between the United States and Italy**

---

**Accordo internazionale di previdenza sociale tra gli Stati Uniti e l'Italia**

U. S. Department of
Health, Education, and Welfare
Social Security Administration
HEW Publication No. (SSA)79-10171
April 1979

This HEW Publication indicates the beginning of the internationalization of our Social Security System with other nations. Other booklets are available with agreements on Social Security with other nations. This agreement with Italy was effective November 1, 1978, according to the HEW Publication noted above. This internationalization is a part of the "666 System," another term for the One World Government.

John Lennon of the Beatles, put it acceptably deceptive:

*"Imagine there's no heaven, it's easy if you try,*
*No hell below us, above us only sky,*
*Imagine all the people, living for today.*

*Imagine there's no countries, it isn't hard to do,*
*Nothing to kill or die for, and no religion too,*
*Imagine all the people, living life in peace.*

*Imagine no possessions, I wonder if you can,*
*No need for greed or hunger, a brotherhood of*
    *man,*
*Imagine all the people, sharing all the world.*

*You may say I'm a dreamer, but I'm not the*
    *only one,*
*I hope someday you'll join us, and the*
    *WORLD will be as ONE."*

Verse #1 destroys all Christian values; no heaven, no hell. Verse #2 destroys love of country and religion. Verse #3 espouses Socialism-Communism.

Oh, Nathan Hale, where are you? We can only faintly recall at the age of 21, you were a school teacher who proudly volunteered to fight for freedom, got caught by the enemy with the goods on you, refused a captaincy in the enemy British ranks, and an ample purse, and were sentenced to die by hanging within 24 hours. You were refused a Bible, and a Chaplain, and even a piece of paper on which to scribble a message, but when you climbed the gallows you orally sent your message around the world. "I only regret that I have but one life to lose for my country."

And Mother England, you are no longer subtle with your mischief. I hurried through a brief stopover in Europe where the number one song by Sex Pistol was,

> *"I am Antichrist, I am Antichrist,*
> *I know what I want, I know how to get it,*
> *I want to destroy."*

I was almost rendered immobile when I heard those words set to music.

Recognizing the depth of the involvement in and the irreversible trend toward One World Socialism, my inner man cries, "Oh, Church of Jesus Christ, where have you been these past 20 years?" And the answer comes resounding back, "On the seashore, the mountains, the lakes, the golf courses." Deuteronomy 8:11-14, comes to mind:

> "Beware that thou forget not the Lord thy God . . . Lest when thou hast eaten and art full, and has built goodly houses, and dwelt therein; And when thy herds and thy flocks multiply, and thy silver and thy gold is multiplied, and all that thou hast is multiplied; Then thine heart be lifted up, and thou forget the Lord thy God."

Yes, we have been "lovers of pleasure more than lovers of God."

> *"If Nero fiddled while Rome burned*
> *America played while the worm turned."*

MSR

## Scriptural Aspects

The One World efforts of Nebuchadnezzar were not thwarted until God made him a "King of Kings," totalitarian ruler over "all men, beasts and fouls," Daniel 2:37, 38, even allowing him to have an image built and requiring the world to worship it . . . for Nebuchadnezzar was the "head of gold," of Daniel 2; and the King of the beasts in Daniel 7. Each subsequent world kingdom not only deteriorated in metal, but also in power. The Medo-Persian Kingdom's strength was divided between the Medes and Persians; it was reduced to a kingdom of silver. The Greek Kingdom's power was further diluted as Alexander the Great had his generals with whom to contend; this was the trunk of brass. The Roman Kingdom was less autocratic for the Caesars had a Senate about which to worry. The ten toes were further deteriorated into iron and clay. What many view as the highest form of government today, a democracy, God views as the lowest. When there is an absolute ruler (as Nebuchadnezzar), if he should turn sour, the people have only to worry about one person; in a democracy, they have to worry about hundreds.

Plato, who alluded to the purest form of government being a benevolent dictatorship, lamented in his Republic, when a state declines to a democracy he means "mere mob rule." *Encyclopedia Americana* "P" — page 238.

No one since *Nebuchadnezzar* has been allowed by God (who both sets up and removes kings, Daniel 2:21) to come near this lofty position held by this ancient Babylonian . . . although many have died trying.

It was a God-ordained prototype from which we *must* learn, as Paul instructed:

> "Now all these things happened unto them for ensamples: and they are written for our admonition, upon whom the ends of the world are come." I Corinthians 10:11.

We are deep in the days of the formation of the 7th World Attempt to govern mankind in peace. History has recorded six great World Kingdoms: Egypt, Assyria, Babylon, Medo-Persia, Greece, and Rome. Rome has never ceased to be a power. When her temporal power was suspended in 1870, she became a spiritual power sending from and receiving official emmisaries at the Vatican. "Five are fallen (Egypt, Assyria, Babylon, Persia and Greece); one (Rome) is; one is to come (the Revived Roman Empire); and the eighth (Antichrist's One World Government) will be of the seventh," the exile, John, penned before the close of the first century. Revelation 17:10-11.

The seventh World Kingdom is the Revived Roman Empire, the nucleus of which we accept as the European Economic Countries, which remained economic until 1979, at which time they became political! For the first time since the days of Charlemagne, *European* elections were held, and only in 1980 have we begun to read about the Europeans (not Germans, not Italians); "A European Budget"; "European arms."

From this seventh World Kingdom consisting of ten major nations will come a World Dictator (most like Nebuchadnezzar) but, much more wicked, receiving his power from the Dragon (Satan).

Perhaps the only good thing a student of Bible Prophecy can say about this One World Government is that it will only endure seven years; the last seven years of this World Order. For,

> "In the days of these (ten) kings shall the God of Heaven set up a Kingdom which shall never be destroyed . . . Then the sovereignty, power and greatness of the kingdoms under the whole heaven will be handed over to the saints . . ." Daniel 2:44; 7:27 NIV.

The Great Prophet, Priest and soon coming King affirmed Daniel's prophecy when he said, "Blessed are the meek, for they shall inherit the earth." Matthew 5:4.

The dye is cast. We are far past the point of no return. The One World Government is upon us.

Oh Christian! Your citizenship is not in Brussels! It is "in heaven from which we look for the Saviour, the Lord Jesus Christ."

## Economic Aspects

> "In a little while . . .I will shake all nations, and the *desire* (silver and gold) of all nations *shall come . . .*" "The treasure of all nations shall come hither." NEB "The treasures of the nations will pour into this temple, and I will fill it with splendor." LB "The silver and gold are mine," saith the Lord, 520 B.C. Haggai 2:6-8.

84

Haggai laments because the restored temple of Zerubbabel was a poor thing compared to the former one which Solomon built; but, the Lord God Almighty, who came "declaring the end from the beginning, and from ancient times the things that are not yet done," comforted the Prophet in modern vernacular thusly; "Wait a little longer, Son; for when I get through shaking the nations, causing their great monetary institutions to fall like Humpty Dumpty, and to flow into Jerusalem, my temple will make Solomon's look like a poor thing!"

Perhaps the most significant and unsuspecting piece in the mosaic of the End Times concerns the collapse of the economics of the world. If fear of annihilation of mankind is used by the politicians to encourage acceptance of the One World Government, then the hope of a leader who can stabilize the collapsing economics of the world and restore value to a currency; though it will be a World Currency, will be used by the economists. Henri Spaak, Secretary-General of NATO, and early planner for the European Common Market said,

> "What we want is a man of sufficient stature to hold the allegiance of all people, and lift us out of the economic morass into which we are sinking. Send us such a man, and whether he be *god or devil,* we will receive him." *Moody Monthly,* March 1974.

On my last missionary trip in the Orient, I found myself being detained a half hour endeavoring to make a $5.00 purchase. Subsequently, I was startled at the refusals of merchants to cash checks, or give advances on my credit cards. I soon learned I was in for a rude awakening. The United States dollar was sliding so drastically against other currencies that besides a reluctance to accept the dollar, it was a humiliating necessity to get a moment by moment quote on its decreasing worth. Only eight months prior I had experienced no such difficulty, so I was totally unprepared for and uninformed of this precarious condition of the dollar before departure from San Francisco. Unable to understand newscasts, I began to pick up newspapers. (English versions.)

*LONDON* (AP), August 20, 1978, London's highly respected *Financial Times* commented . . . ''Without effective intervention in the foreign exchange markets, *the dollar could topple* at the *next bit of bad news.''*

*THE CHINA NEWS,* August 19, 1978, Washington, D.C. (AP) — ''The United States must be ready to intervene in world money markets to prop up the falling dollar, United States Senator Jacob Javits told the Senate Thursday . . . *The World monetary system eventually will be restructured* in a way that would gradually replace reliance on the dollar . . . this new arrangement will make the monetary system more responsive to *international financial reality.''*

*TOKYO* (AP), ''The yen Friday closed at 186 against the dollar. Some industries won't be able to survive if the United States dollar falls to the 180 yen level.''

*THE CHINA NEWS,* August 21, 1978, ''United States pledges more action to support sagging $ (dollar).''

Many times circumstances dictate God's will . . . day by day I lived cognizant that if the ''dollar toppled,'' negating my ability to make traveling arrangements, I would be a long term missionary to the Chinese!

Returning to the United States, I found virtually no one aware of the crisis in our monetary policy, and received no sympathy at all for my anxieties experienced abroad. I learned that the Republic of China indeed has a ''free press''; and, I was much better informed about the sad posture of our dollar than my colleagues who had been at home reading the ''approved version'' of the news.

Only a few years prior, I had piloted my twin throughout Central America being met at almost every stop by the poor with outstretched hands begging for ''American dollar, please?''

I become fraught with emotion when I realize what has happened to the American dollar, and subsequently, the United States' economy. I become more disturbed when I must acknowledge the United States is not an isolated case. The monetary units and economies of the world are all ''in a ditch.''

# Economic Morass

A line in one of my old history books comes to mind. ''The surest way to overthrow an established Social order is to debauch its currency.'' Nikolai Lenin, *Russian Bolshevist Revolutionary, 1910.*

*U.S. News and World Report,* October 29, 1979, indicated the dollar was worth 24ᶜ predicated upon the 1945 dollar being worth 100 cents — which it wasn't. *The dollar hasn't been worth 100 cents since 1933 when it was removed* from the gold standard and one *could exchange a $5.00 bill* for a $5.00 gold piece.

''The most serious problem we face today is the debasement of our currency by the government. The government will continue to debase the dollar until . . . within 12-24 months it will shrink to 1ᶜ . . . at which time Washington will be forced to create the *new hard currency . . .* it will take at least $100 to buy one new dollar. A currency reform is nothing but a fancy name for state bankruptcy; . . . this currency reform will be imposed with swiftness and brutality. A currency reform completes the expropriation of all kinds of savings . . . it will wipe out all public and private bonds, most pensions, all annuities, and all endowments . . . do not store your silver and gold in a safe deposit box . . . Devaluations generally take place over a weekend. There is a chance that one historic Monday the box will have a red seal on it and may be opened only in the presence of Government Agents.''

Dr. Franz Pick, renowned World Currency Authority, late December 1979, *Silver and Gold Report.*

Julian Snyder says in *International Money Line,* February 1978,

"The United States is trying to solve its problem through currency depreciation (debasement) . . . it will not work. If the crash does not occur this year, it could be postponed until 1982."

Some economists, and men of great expertise in World Currencies, are in agreement for the first time, that the dollar could become obsolete within two years, and all paper currencies in four to five years.

In the *Robbin's Report,* January 15, 1978, Mr. Robbins says, "Look for hyperinflation and collapse of all the *world's paper money before 1985.*"

Bill Newkirk reporting for the AP said recently:

*"A new World Exchange System which will dominate the economies of nations for the next 25 years is but months away."*

The real worth of the dollar has been posted at as little as 6 cents. It cannot go much lower before the Government will have to declare *default* on its tremendous debt, and start over with a new currency. Oh, yes, we are listening to the countdown for the medium of exchange which has held this great United States' Economy together, the dollar. It is now T minus .06 and counting.

I was privileged to spend some hours with a most respected Christian friend, Willard Cantelon, in June 1980. He very emphatically declared that "as surely

89

as the Deutchmark was cancelled in Germany in 1923 and 1946, the dollar will be cancelled!''

Other astute contemporaries have been declaring the end of our system. T. Coleman Andrews, IRS Official as far back as 1961, said, ''I defy man or devil to say that the dollar can survive more than a few years.'' Soon afterwards, George Humphrey, Secretary of Treasury, declared, ''We are on the verge of something that will curl a man's hair to think about it. It will make the depression of the 1930's look like rip roaring prosperity.''

Eliot Janeway, renowned economist said in *Esquire,* November 21, 1978; ''If we can't get interest rates down, it's going to make 1929 look like a prosperous lawn party.''

In the mid 1970's, *World Bank,* Paper 447 Article 3, predicts the economies of the world to remain fairly stable until about 1980, beyond which time they see them falling in domino fashion. Is there any wonder Ludwig Erhart, Finance Minister of Germany, following World War II would decry,

''Give us problems, or give us depression, but do not give us inflation, for it is the sure eventual death to every economy.''

Dear Reader, ''the *letter* killeth, but the spirit maketh alive . . . 'yet' my people perish for the *lack of knowledge.*'' So please hang in here a few minutes and let me explain the common term inflation to you so that you may know that:

1. Our government is past the point of no return.
2. Our dollar is doomed for an early demise.
3. Our economy will collapse!

"His truth shall be my shield and buckler"; our protection! Truth is not only *protective,* it is *directive.* We are closing in on the time when it will be knowledge or perish; and since knowledge has been increased, "to whom much is given (knowledge), much is required." There will be those who stick their heads in the sand, and become the first to jump out tenth story windows when things get tough. The truth is — the bridge *is out* a few miles down the road — and if you are warned before you get there, you won't hit the water making 60 mph. You will reassess your directions and choose an alternate course.

Let me assure you now that Jesus Christ spanned that bridge *for you.* "Though he was rich, yet for your sakes he became poor, that ye through his poverty might be rich." When the money failed in Egypt and the Egyptians (the world) bartered their flocks and their land and finally "sold their souls to the company store (Pharoah)," the Israelites (God's children) were placed in the *best of the land, nourished,* and *made rulers!* Genesis 47:6, 11, 12, 15. "NOW ALL THESE HAPPENED UNTO THEM FOR ENSAMPLES (types) AND THEY ARE WRITTEN FOR *OUR* ADMONITION UPON WHOM THE *ENDS* OF THE WORLD ARE COME." I Corinthians 10:11.

## Inflation = Debasement = Deficit Spending

"Inflated" means to be swollen or pumped up with gas — a stretching of the original material without any increase in substance. Inflation is to the public an increase in prices, but this is only a result. It is to the economist, an increase in the supply of money.

Milton Friedman, *Nobel Laureate, Book Digest,* May 1980,

> "dismisses the *conventional reasons* for runaway inflation and identifies it as the *printing presses* of the United States Mint . . . greedy businessmen, grasping trade unions, spend thrift consumers, Arab sheiks, bad weather . . . can produce high prices . . . causing *temporary* ups and downs in the rate of inflation, but they *cannot produce* inflation for one simple reason, none of the alleged culprits possess a *printing press.* Financing government spending by increasing the quantity of money is extremely attractive to both the President and members of Congress. It enables them to *increase government spending* providing goodies for their constituents, without having to vote for taxes to pay for them and without having to borrow from the public. Financing government spending by increasing the quantity of money looks like magic, like getting something for nothing."

The government simply creates money by printing it, then spending it, lending it, or giving it away. This is debasement which causes inflation.

From 1870 to 1933, the dollar was on the gold standard. When a currency is backed by a hard currency, there is a built-in discipline and the government cannot manipulate the currency. In 1933, President Roosevelt accepted the advice of Englishman John Maynard Keynes who insisted that deficit spending would be like a shot of adrenalin in the heart of the economy. This required removing the dollar from the gold standard, which allowed the government to begin the slow, but sure process of debasing the dollar.

James Dines said,

> "Today's crisis has been building since 1933. There has been no precedent for such monetary instability in the financial history of the world. The man on the street has no concept of the financial panic which could lie just before us." *The Invisible Crash (New York, Ballantine,* page 5)

Gold was required to be turned in to the government @ $20.67 an ounce. Immediately its value was increased to $35.00 an ounce, producing some three billion dollars profit for the government. What happens, however, when the price of gold increases? The value of the dollar comes down.

In 1934, our government began to print more dollars (without any increase in substance), and spend them. For 34 out of the past 37 years, our Congress has approved deficit federal budgets which required the printing of additional dollars to finance the deficits.

(Try to think of a family which in 1934 had an income of $10,000, but, spent $13,000, so they borrowed the needed $3,000. In 1935, they had an income of $14,000, but, they spent $18,000; so they borrowed another $4,000 and paid interest on the $3,000. Note here they paid nothing on the old loan, but just serviced the debt. In 1936, their income was $16,000, but, they spent $21,000. They borrowed their deficit spending of $5,000 and paid interest on the old deficit of $7,000. If this family had followed this fiscal policy of spending more than their income each year since 1933, except for four years when they lived within their budget, in what kind of financial condition would this family be? *This is the posture of our Federal Government except each year they just printed more dollars to pay* for their reckless spending — unlegislated taxation.) Our national debt which must be serviced is now 893 billion. *Spotlight,* July 21, 1980, page 29.

Dow Theory Letters, Inc., wrote a detailed report recently showing that by *1982* the cost of servicing the national debt *"would eat* up *all the government tax money available!"*

Dr. H.A. Murkline, Director of International Institute, University of Dallas in Irving, Texas, wrote in *World Oil 1976,* that according to his projections, the longest time that the Federal Government could possibly remain viable would be the close of the fiscal year 1981.

I have to believe that if the Federal Government *Officials knew that* the citizens *understood* that every time they approve a *deficit budget,* they are debasing our dollars, they would shape up with some semblance of fiscal sanity. By the same measure they overspend, the citizens experience inflation. Inflation is inversely proportional to deficit spending . . . allowing a little lag time.

I watched "Wall Street Week in Review," March 21, 1980, on which the Chairman of the Board of Merril Lynch was the guest. A panelist posed this question to him, "What effect does the doubling of the cost of oil since 1973 have on our present inflation rate?" The reply was, "*virtually nothing*. Inflation is nothing more or less than government deficit spending; . . . there might be a temporary factor of 1.8% of our 20% inflation rate at this moment attributable to the increase in the oil price."

Now with some understanding that the cause of inflation is deficit spending, which since 1934 has swollen our national debt, and the cost of *servicing* it annually, one would think only an imbecile would approve any more deficit spending. Not so. Here is an article which appeared in the *New York Times,* March 6, 1980.

"The Congressional Budget Office expects a $46 billion deficit in the Federal budget for the current fiscal year, six billion more than the Carter Administration said a month ago. Congress *already has* exceeded its spending limit 10 billion . . . Debate on several bills, including *large appropriations* for the *WORLD BANK,* aid for Nicaragua, and Cambodia was immediately suspended."

# Inflation's Subtle Blows

Let me digress to ask and answer one question. "Do you know what determines the interest rate on our money?" It is determined by the demands made on the supply. "Do you know *now* who is making the tremendous demands on our supply?" *Yes, the Feds!* They must have it at any cost to service this huge debt or the United States Government would be bankrupt. Consequently, the Feds have caused the interest rates to rise so high that the businessman cannot compete with them for money and pay 20%, so the business community (economy) of the United States is sinking deeper and deeper into recession; and *as long as this national debt increases, the economy must decrease.* Yet, there is no way of balancing the budget with the gross inequities and mis-management of our present government officials.

*Time,* December 24, 1979, was right on.

> "The decade will open with an economy turned sour, an energy problem unsolved, and a menacing international situation."

And so was *U.S. News & World Report,* December 31, 1979,

> "Ahead for America stretches a somber, pivotal, and hectic 1980."

James Doyle, *UPI,* stated:

> "The world's largest bank, a noted International banking economics division, and a prestigeous forecast center agree, 'The economy

will start out bad and get worse.' ''

Inflation has reached such galloping proportions that Henry Kaufman, held in awe by the financial community, *Time,* March 10, 1980, said:

"Declare a National Emergency."

Alan Greenspan, a principal advisor to Presidents Nixon and Ford, warns that:

"We have a window of but six months to bring inflation to heel." *U.S. News & World Report,* March 17, 1980, page 92.

Some of President Carter's top appointees share the gloomy assessments of the future,

*"It will be devastating, absolutely terrifying,"* says Charles Warren, Chairman of President Carter's Council of Environmental Quality when asked about the future of the economy. *San Jose Mercury,* May 29, 1979.

"Around the cluttered White House offices last week, a new term was being uttered in often hushed terms; hyperinflation. Price rises can no longer be easily labeled creeping or even galloping. Said one nervous Carter aide: 'People in meetings are really talking about hyperinflation.' '' *Time,* March 10, 1980.

### History's Hyperinflations

The Roman Emperor, Diocletian, about 300 A.D., sent runners throughout the kingdom with these instructions:

> "Hurry and spend all the currency you have. Buy me goods of any kind at whatever price you find them . . . for prices are increasing not only year by year, but month by month, day by day, hour by hour, and moment by moment."

> "Germany, between World War I and II, suffered a four trillion percent inflation." *Time,* March 10, 1980.

In 1914, the mark was stable and a pound of butter sold for one and one/half marks. In 1918, a pound of butter sold for three marks; creeping inflation. (The German Government had printed twice as many marks as they had in 1914.) In the spring of 1922, a pound of butter sold for 2400 marks (galloping inflation). In the summer of 1922, a pound of butter sold for 150,000 marks (hyperinflation); and in the Fall of 1922, a pound of butter sold for six billion marks (1.5 million American dollars). The government began to print marks in million mark denominations; but, it still meant hauling marks to the market in wheelbarrows to buy a loaf of bread that sold for 168 billion marks. A German banker said, "We stopped counting them, we put them on scales and weighed them." Wages were advancing by the hour. While Germans were having dinner in restaurants, they were aware the price of their dinners would escalate two or three times. This Deutschmark was cancelled in 1923.

My Bible has 1500 pages in it. Can you imagine having to count each page of a Bible to purchase a loaf of bread? The Germans had to count 268,000 marks (if they were all in one million denominations)! You can see how Christians who do not submit to the Electronic Money System (see that chapter) will be ostracized in times of hyperinflation. Think of the convenience of a single card with a number and the inconvenience of hauling millions of dollars to the market place for a loaf of bread, where the merchant will resent having to assist you.

> "Economists differ in their explanation of how a country leaves simply galloping inflation and enters the stratosphere of hyperinflation . . . But all agree there is some inflation flashpoint at which people become convinced that prices will never stop rising and lose all confidence in their currency. Says former Federal Reserve Chairman Arthur Burns: 'At that time, it appears that anything is better than holding money. People start putting everything into any tangible good they can find.' " *Time,* March 10, 1980.

History's greatest inflation was experienced in Hungary in 1946, when prices rose 20,000% monthly. It took one hundred million trillion pengo bills to be worth $10.00. The important question is, "How near are we to this inflation flashpoint, at which time all goods are bought up in a few days; hyperinflation, and cancellation of the dollar by our government?"

> "European Economists *today* are calling the dollar, 'Printing Press Money.' This was a term used in Germany when the inflated

Deutschmark was used as fuel for the fire.''
*The Day The Dollar Dies,* Willard Cantelon.

## Mismanagement Has Surfaced

Many innocent, uninformed, even non-voters will suffer greatly as a result of our carelessly elected representatives' poor fiscal policies. The suffering will be deeper and sooner for our not having been informed earlier so that demands for fiscal reforms could have been made before we reached the point of no return.

1. The Feds felt it necessary to withhold the mailout of income tax refund checks amounting to three billion dollars for fear the United States Treasury would bounce (April 1980).

2. The Feds delayed mailing out the Social Security checks for June 3, 1980; insufficient funds.

3. ''There are 29,000 employees on the Federal level gathering statistics in 100 different agencies, costing one billion dollars a year simply to accumulate data.'' *Montgomery Advertiser,* July 19, 1980.

4. The predictions by government officials are that Social Security could be bankrupt in late 1981 or early 1982. ''Social Security,'' said an official, ''has $3.75 trillion dollars worth of IOU's out. These would have to be paid if Social Security were to shut down tomorrow.'' *Montgomery Advertiser,* July 19, 1980. *The San Jose Mercury,* September 18, 1980, ran an article entitled, ''Social Security chief says fund broke in a year.''

If this bleak outlook for millions of deserving, law abiding citizens isn't paltry enough, *Social Security benefits are still being paid to 30,000 murderers, including Son of Sam sentenced to 300 years* (since which time he's received $500,000 for movie rights on his life), and to Carl Eckstrom, convicted of murdering four persons in Florida, and to rapists, robbers and deviates whose Social Security benefits average between $300-$400 per month. This should not just be classified mis-management, but fraud against millions of legitimate Social Security beneficiaries.

## Is Your Money Really Safe?

Perhaps the greatest delusion under which the American people are laboring is that their money in FDIC insured accounts is safe.

*The Spotlight,* June 2, 1980, reported that when First Pennsylvania Bank of Philadelphia, the nation's twenty-third largest bank failed (technically) in May 1980, the FDIC, Federal Reserve Board, and United States Comptroller of Currency, unable to work out an agreement between the ailing and a healthier financial institution, because of the size of its liabilities, pressured 23 of the nations largest banks to accept the responsibilities, ''which saved it from a major disaster that could have rocked the entire United States and International Banking System.'' A Federal Reserve spokesman said, ''If *one or two* more insolvencies the size of First Pennsylvania take place, they can literally wipe out FDIC and create one of the greatest panics

101

and bank runs this world has ever seen. There would be nothing left." Frank Skillern, Legal Division FDIC, said, "The FDIC was not conceived to handle a situation of the type that occurred in the 1929 crash . . . moreover he indicated that a financial collapse was a real possibility." He acknowledged that the *basic functions* of the bank regulatory system . . . are to a *great degree psychological* because they create a "perception of security" for the saver.

*The Christian Science Monitor,* July 29, 1980, carried an article asking the question, "How safe are US savings accounts?" It stated that: "The FDIC is not alone in its limited level of insurance protection: At the Federal Savings and Loan Corporation (FSLIC), which insures savings and loan associations, the agency's $6 billion in reserves also equals only about $1 per $100 of deposits."

FDIC is reported to have had $6 billion insuring $628 billion in 1978. In 1980, the figure is reported to be $10 billion insuring in excess of a trillion dollars. In synopsis, the increase in FDIC insurance from $40,000 to $100,000 is a "come on" to persuade investors to leave their money in the banks so that the Fed can make use of it right to the time of catastrophe, which will occur when inflation wipes out the dollar, and devaluation or cancellation will result *in the event we are, or are not in the Electronic Money System at this time.* (See that chapter.)

It is wise to remember the exchange rates used historically of new currency for old. In recent years, Brazil exchanged 1000 old cruzeiros for one new one. Greece exchanged 1000 old for one new drachma.

France used a 100 to 1 franc exchange ratio. Almost *every* South American country has had to reform its currency system since World War II, while over a hundred nations around the world have devalued their currency, some many times. "It is not worth a Continental," came from the fact that Secretary of Treasury Hamilton finally redeemed 100 Continental dollars for one new dollar.

## The New Banking Act

The new Banking Act passed in March 1980, requires all 40,000 banks to join the Federal Reserve System. Until then, only about 4,600 were members. *The Christian Science Monitor* of July 29, 1980, alludes to the "Monetary Control Act of 1980 as 'Big Brother' comes to the banking system."

"Senator Robert Morgan (DNC) predicted massive failures of Savings & Loans Institutions along with other small banks upon its enactment." It is also the vital link that will "blend United States currency with foreign currencies into a *World Currency.* This movement toward worldwide currency fits in with what National Security Advisor Brzezinski states as a Trilateral Commission goal several years ago. At the end of the road is an America which is just *one industrial state among many* in the West where a unified currency is used which is controlled by International bankers through the Fed." *Spotlight,* April 28, 1980.

As surely as we are enveloped in a National banking crisis, of which we need to be apprised, we are equally affected by and need to be informed of the International banking crisis, from which we can learn what has happened to citizens' money in banks when cancellation or devaluation of currency has occurred in other nations.

Brazil, the most indebted of all the Lesser Developed Countries is in debt to Western banks 50 billion dollars. They must borrow 15 billion in 1980 to service the debt.

> "If Brazil is denied the 15 billion requests and the banks call the loan in default, some of them call themselves (their own banks) into bankruptcy. Further, if the United States banks, responsible for at least 55 billion (in loans to lesser developed countries) ring the bell, it will surely start the dominos falling to produce the greatest financial disaster in history." C.V. Myers, of *Myers Finance Energy Newsletter*.

Devaluation of currency took place early in 1980 in Brazil, "without warning, the government cancelled early withdrawal privileges freezing all deposits . . ." states *Business Week,* April 7, 1980.

The most respected Mr. Donald Hoppe, in his recent newsletter (P.O. Box 513, Crystal Lake, Illinois 60014) said:

> "Events are now moving so swiftly that a major breakdown in the world's economic and financial structure should be anticipated

104

within the next two years . . . All that can be said for sure is, (1) that things cannot go on much longer as they are, and (2) that no one in authority appears to have any idea of how financial equilibrium and international monetary stability can be restored . . . Thus we are poised between a massive international debt default and banking crisis, which would obviously be drastically deflationary and result in a severe world depression . . .''

A man of great expertise, Mr. R.E. McMasters, writing in *The Reaper* (P.O. Box 39026, Phoenix, Arizona 85069) stated:

"The American banking system is as vulnerable today as it was in the early 1930's. Only 66% of the banks in this country are in satisfactory condition according to the Federal Reserve . . . Please recall that the last time (73-74) the banking industry faced a liquidity crisis, Franklin National Bank failed. Its demise almost toppled the banking system and came within a gnat's eyelash of triggering a run on the banks . . .''

In the *Wall Street Journal,* February 20, 1980, astute men like David Rockefeller, Chairman, Chase Manhattan Bank forecast, ''Treacherous economic seas and gale force winds.'' And Mr. Otto Emminger, retired Chief of West Germany's Central Bank fears that ''the whole structure could, like Humpty Dumpty, have a great fall.''

There seems to be no solution to the problem, only

delay, as we wait for the New World Order, which could be as AP's Mr. Neurkirk says, "Only months away."

## The New Money

"For over a *decade* bankers and technicians of Europe had been feverishly working to establish a new number system that would replace the antiquated currencies that were plaguing the international-trade world with confusion," says Willard Cantelon in *New Money or None.*

Although we are very near the implementation of this new number system (see chapter Electronic Money Society), there must be some standardized unit of exchange by which monetary values can be fixed.

Should anyone be surprised that the European Economic Countries have already accomodated the world with the introduction of this new money?

"On March 13, 1979, an event of signal importance for Europe went almost unreported by the American media: the founding, under the auspices of the Parliament of Europe — the governing body of the European Economic Community — of the new European Monetary System. On that date, in Strasbourg, France, the nine countries of the Common Market laid the groundwork for a common European currency." *Low Mintage Club Report, Volume III, No. 9,* October 1979.

"THE NEW MONEY," the "ECU," European Currency Unit.

The ECU (European Currency Unit) is backed by fully 20% of the participating countries' gold reserves, 3,150 tons. These European Countries will not only distinguish themselves with their World Dictator, but also with their World Currency. The ECU's will surely become the One World Currency, by which all other currencies are weighed until they cease to exist. Prior to this time, each person in the world will be assigned a number inscribed on the magnetic tape back of a thin plastic card which will ease the pain of the death of the dollar and all the world's paper currencies.

## The Majority Know

I read in *Business Week,* March 24, 1980, these sobering statements: "The economy has been in perilous condition for months. President Carter's proposed fiscal 1981 budget revisions were designed in large measure to restore order to financial markets and to prevent an *imminent collapse of the economy.*" I wondered, "How many Americans are really cognizant that we are experiencing the collapse of the world's once most vaunted economy?" The question was largely answered in *Time,* April 14, 1980; "The number of people who think that the United States is in serious trouble has swelled to 81%." In the same issue there was an article entitled, "Corporate Bankruptcies Head For a New High."

## No Island to Ourselves

*"Of all sad words of tongue or pen,*
*The saddest are these, it might have been . . ."*

It might have been only a national problem with just the United States economy involved; but, the unique thing about inflation (the eventual death to every economy) is that in this decade of the 1980's, it is a worldwide phenomenon! Someone wiser than I coined "when America sneezes, the world takes a cold." Since the economy of the United States now has pneumonia, how sick are the economies of the world?

"Internationally there is an 'absolutely new development.' Bonn's (Germany's) big plusses in dealings abroad are over." *U.S. News and World Report,* April 14, 1980. The article further stated that "West Germany suffered a five billion deficit in 1979, and is looking at a 12 billion deficit in 1980.

"The business outlook in Europe is turning gloomier than in the United States. . . . But, it's what comes later in 1981-82 that really has them worried. . . . The gravest threat comes from uncontrolled inflation. America's flaring prices are by no means unique. Europe's latest prices are alarming with increases at an annual rate of 21.5% in January and February for the Nine Nation Common Market, and as much as 26.5% in Britain, and 31.7% in Italy." Unless inflation is halted, the alternative is seen as a risk of financial collapse. "The 1980's could be a decade of permanent crisis." *U.S. News & World Report,* April 14, 1980.

What we read of the Socialist economies sounds no better. The first strike occurred in Russia in June 1980, at an auto plant. The workers complained of insufficient meat and bread. Cuba is reported in *Newsweek,* March 3, 1980, as receiving $10 million *per day* from Russia to prop up her ailing economy, but in spite of this infusion, her crops are rotting in the fields, and her factories are closing down.

The editor of the *London Times,* William Ress-Mogg, published a book recently entitled *The Crisis of*

*World Inflation,* in which he makes these statements:

"Ruin and revolution are the consequence of inflation. There is no inflation which has not started with an increase in the money supply and there is no inflation which has not ended with a corruption of society proportionate only to the degree of inflation that society experienced. . . . Inflation causes men to take short views."

"When a nation's currency is healthy," he said, "men plant oak trees. When a nation's currency is debauched," he said, "men plant cabbage." This book indicates that currency in nation after nation is becoming worthless and, he says, that unless inflation is curbed riot and world revolution will result.

Willard Cantelon says, "There is not a conversant person in the world with whom I have spoken who would argue that the *world* is presently beyond the point of no return. No longer is the question, 'Is a new system coming?' The question now is only *WHEN.*"

## It Will Get Worse

So we see the giant wheels of commerce grinding slowly to a halt as economy after economy succumbs to the innocent sounding term "inflation." It is not my purpose to criticize any person, official, or institution; just to inform you that it has been brought on mankind by greedy, power hungry governments, which have chosen the one method (debasing the currency), most misunderstood by the people to bring the economies to the brink of chaos.

Oh, that I could say that the glow is on the horizon, and better days are ahead. They are, but, not before they get worse.

> "History's great inflations have almost always been followed by a dictator who promised among other things to restore the currency's value. Napoleon, Hitler and Mao Tsetung all rode to power on the back of hyperinflation." *Time*, March 10, 1980.

As I have said, there is a unique aspect about inflation in the 1980's; it is worldwide in scope.

I predict that: (1) The next development in the formation of the One World Government will be galloping inflation worldwide, followed in quick succession by hyperinflation. Inflations significant to historians of the past, as Rome, France, Germany and Hungary will be totally eclipsed by the inflation our world is about to experience. (This hyperinflation will be the tool used to get peoples and nations to submit to the Electronic Money System.)

(2) When the economies of the world start falling in domino fashion, there will be a person rising from the European Community to begin picking up the pieces. Unfortunately, he will not be another Sir Winston Churchill, or General Dwight Eisenhower, but, Sir Satan Incarnate, Mr. 666, the "Other Christ."

> Oh Jeremiah, how correct you were; "it is not in man that walketh to direct his steps," Jeremiah 10:23. Jesus affirmed it, "if the

111

blind lead the blind, both shall fall into the ditch.'' Matthew 15:14.

The world has been totally devoid of positive leadership for years, and even more devoid of spiritual leadership! Oh! for a King David, a man after God's own heart; or a King Hezekiah, who chose a session with a prophet of God prior to mapping out a defense strategy! Or, just an Abe Lincoln, who started each day on his knees before God. In the absence of such leadership, the whole world is in the ditch.

But, Christians, take heart . . . this entire regime of the Antichrist will last only seven years, at which time King Jesus shall come back (''with all the saints with him'' Zechariah 14:5) and ''cast both the beast and the false prophet *alive* into a lake of fire.'' Revelation 19:20.

In the interim, God is going to shake the treasuries of the nations, and the gold and silver that have held the economies of the world together will begin to flow into Jerusalem, where it will be used to adorn the Temple which King Jesus shall build himself (Acts 15:16; Haggai 2:6-8): from which headquarters he shall take upon himself the reins of the government, and upon the door of His Majesty's house will be inscribed his titles: ''WONDERFUL, COUNSELOR, THE MIGHTY GOD, THE EVERLASTING FATHER, THE PRINCE OF PEACE,'' and, ''of the increase (abundance — surplus, no more deficits) of His Government and *Peace* there shall be no end. His dominion shall be from sea to sea and from the river to the ends of the earth. And the earth shall be full of the knowledge of the Lord as the waters cover the sea.''

112

Isaiah 9:6-7; 11:9; Zechariah 9:10.

Yes,

> *"It shall flow like a river, it shall fall like the*
> *rain,*
> *It shall rise at the dawning, in glory o're the*
> *land;*
> *And the knowledge of the Lord, shall fill all*
> *the earth,*
> *And the spirit of the Lord will fall."*

## Some Do's and Don't's

1. Don't owe your soul to the Antichrist. Some evangelists are advocating that people buy everything they desire and leave the debts to the Antichrist. In the first place, this is unscriptural. "Owe no man anything except to love him." And, there is II Thessalonians 2:3, which makes it very clear that Christians will be here at the beginning of this last seven year period and indeed when he will be revealed. Since he will make war with the saints. (Daniel 7:21&25; Revelation 13:7) the fewer financial transactions required will be the better.

2. Pay all debts that you can. (Inflation is on the debtor's side; but, debts are not scripturally recommended.) When the crash comes, you will only own that which is paid for. Your salvation was paid for 2,000 years ago . . . "Be very sure your anchor holds and grips the solid rock." His name is Jesus Christ.

3. Pay off your home mortgage if you have savings sufficient. There is no reciprocity in banks. If you have a $20,000 Certificate of Deposit in one department of

a bank, and owe a $10,000 mortgage to another department; if the bank closes, you would lose your Certificate of Deposit, but the bank could repo your home.

4. If possible, buy an acre of land out of the city. Put a tent, trailer, or cottage there; raise a garden, learn to can, dig a well; and learn to live independent of city conveniences.

5. Give abundantly to the Lord's work. He will not be a debtor to anyone. I have given about 80% of my income for years to works raised up by God around the world. I believe in the local church. Remember, tithes and offerings are to be given on your income, but stewardship has to do with how you invest your assets.

6. Pray for guidance to know in what to convert your liquid assets. Silver, gold, groceries, or land would have more value than cancelled dollars. Many recommend you own a bag of silver coins for each member of your family. Some will lament, ''But silver and gold have gone so high!'' No! Silver has remained fairly constant. In 1969, a loaf of bread cost a silver dime or 1/10 of a paper dollar. In 1979, a loaf of bread could still be purchased for a silver dime, but it cost 80% of a paper dollar. In 1979, a $100,000 house could still be purchased for 10,000 silver dollars. The great change hasn't been in silver, but in the paper dollar.

7. Get in the explicit will of God. I believe if you are unable to do any of the foregoing things, but, you are implementing God's will daily, He will ''preserve you, spirit, soul and body unto the coming of the Lord Jesus Christ.''

# CHAPTER IV

# "1984" EARLY?

"And it was given unto him to make war with the saints, and to overcome them: and power was given him over all kindreds, and tongues, and nations. And all that dwell upon the earth shall worship him, whose names are not written in the book of life of the Lamb slain from the foundation of the world." Revelation 13:7-8.

*Immediately after* the Tribulation of those days . . . then shall appear the sign of the Son of Man in Heaven . . . and he shall send his angels . . . and they shall *gather together* His elect from the four winds. Matthew 24:29-31.

This is the "Catching Away"; if it were the Revelation of Christ in Revelation 19 and Zechariah 14:5, "all His saints would be with him."

Since the saints will be here during the first three and one-half years (Tribulation, but not the Wrath of God, the last three and one-half years), let us look at the ways the Antichrist will utilize to "control" mankind.

Buying and selling will be done electronically through video-telephone networks. There will be no banks to hold-up, no cash in purse — no robberies, no cards to lose or steal. The number is on each person's head which can't be borrowed. Kidnapping will be a thing of the past; the ink used by the laser gun to imprint the number on the body will emit approximately one watt, sufficient to allow the computer to trace its location, even on airplanes. The Antichrist and the False Prophet will declare: no more crime, no more war, "Peace and Safety."

In 1948, a secular writer, George Orwell, wrote an imaginary novel and called it *1984*. It depicts the entire world being mercilessly controlled by a government, Big Brother, even to the thought life of each individual. If a person allows his thoughts to depart from subjects sanctioned by Big Brother, the Thought Police are dispatched to discipline him.

A recent survey of scientists indicated 80% of his prophecies had come true already, and "1984" was right on schedule.

## The * and the # Sign on Your Telephone

When the engineers designed the "touch tone telephones" two decades ago, they were instructed to include two "mystery" buttons; the asterisk (*) on the lower left, and the pound sign (#) on the lower right. The asterisk will be pressed to connect each person with the "banking" computer. The pound sign will be used to assist us in pushing in the desired amounts of purchases which we need to transfer from our account to another account.

For over a year in many banks, including some in the Montgomery area, employees pick up their telephones, press the asterisk, and it connects them with the central *banking* computer for Alabama.

## Your TV Is Now Monitoring You!

The home system is waiting for the television hookup. Shopping in the controlled society will be done via television and telephone. For years now, in some larger department stores, when the cashier scans the product number with the infra-red gun, it sends the message to release the product just purchased and previously packaged for the electronic system. It deducts this product from store inventory, and when this stock number gets so low, it automatically sends a message to the warehouse to re-supply the item. In addition, it does all bookkeeping at the same moment, entering price sold at, less cost, yielding gross profit on the store sales journal.

Most of the control over our private lives will be made possible by the television. Televisions will monitor work, earnings, food eaten, leisure hours, and programs watched. They will store in memory banks the analysis of each person's days; how many hours of secular versus religious television one watches; responses to political candidates' speeches and, of course, *how one votes.*

For the persons who feel this is going to take place in some nebulus time called the future, allow me to inform you, this communication capability is now with us, and is being implemented rapidly in parts of the United States.

*THE ULTIMATE TV SET: IT SHOPS, BUYS, TEACHES,* as reported and written by Associate Editor Ronald A. Taylor in the *U.S. News and World Report,* says:

"Television is becoming more than a vehicle for news and entertainment. Before long, the family set may well be the key to information of nearly every sort — from algebra lessons to restaurant menus. In this experiment called Viewtron, some 150 homes in Coral Gables will be equipped with Viewdata, a system that uses telephone lines to link television sets with computer data banks. Using a hand-held signal device, consumers will relay their requests to the computer and receive on their screens shopping information, news, travel schedules, home-study courses, games and more. Viewdata and Bell Telephone Company are sponsoring the test free of charge to see if the idea will be as acceptable in the United States as it has been in Western Europe, where similar systems have been in operation for several months. Viewdata officials say that the system could be particularly useful in areas where people must drive long distances to reach stores. They reason that, as energy problems worsen, families may welcome a system that lets them shop without leaving their homes. With Viewtron, more than 12,000 'pages' of information will be available from the computer 18 hours each day. To retrieve the data they want, users press one of eleven buttons on their control device. A decoder in their television set will then receive the information from the computer. For example, a list of an area's Italian restaurants could be called up on the television screen, complete with current menus and latest prices. Consumers also will be able to call up limited catalogs from department stores as well as prices from a supermarket, a book store, a ticket outlet and caterer. PLACING AN ORDER: To make a purchase, a consumer will fill out a purchase order appearing on the screen by punching a second electronic device that resembles the keyboard of a typewriter. The request is then relayed to the merchant. Also to be offered are adult-education courses in Spanish and other subjects. Again, users will respond to lessons on the screen by punching the keyboard. There will be some problem about this 'invasion of privacy.' ''

In *Contemporary Magazine, Denver Post:* September 10, 1978, there was an article entitled ''Our TV SETS MAY WATCH US.'' by Les Brown, *New York Times* writer. He says:

''George Orwell's prophecy of an advanced electronic society in 1984, in which the *television set may watch as well as be watched, could be right on schedule.* In the next five or six years, a substantial part of the country may be served by a form of two-way cable television that is linked to a set of computers. These computers, sweeping each subscribing household every six or seven seconds, can take orders for merchandise purchased during television commercials, provide burglar and fire alarm protection, read gas and water meters, take public-opinion polls, etc. But desirable, as these services may be — *and most of them already are being offered in Columbus, Ohio,* on Warner Communications futuristic cable system known as Qube, the form of television that provides them raises some difficult questions in a free society. *For the computer also records what every household is watching, and buying, and how each household votes in a poll.* To the extent that computerized television 'watches' the household, even as the viewer is watching the screen, it presumably can be regarded as *invading a citizen's privacy.* A political candidate would find his or her campaign devastated, for example, if computer records that fell into the hands of an opponent should reveal excessive viewing of erotic or pornographic films.''

However, the real lure that will be used to require installation in each household in city after city is that it will make cities *safe* and *efficient* with a fraction of the present personnel and expenses!

# Control Your Thermostats?

In addition to monitoring our activities, this system will regulate and control the consumption of our utilities.

Rowland Stiteler of Dallas, wrote an article entitled "Look At What Is Coming Into Your Living Room."

"One fifty-six A.M. It is quiet in the command post. Two members of the security force sit motionless, staring into a bank of a dozen television screens. They have been trained to be alert for anomalies in the community; anything which threatens security will be sensed electronically in seconds. The Computer tells them that most of the residents are asleep. The guards can see *which doors are open — or closed. The Computer can tell them instantly if a fire is developing in any of the domiciles. It tells them if someone needs medical help, and when someone **has set his thermostat too high or too low**. It has the capability to monitor, **and even control,** electrical consumption in every sector.* The *Community functions like one giant living organism:* The Computer is its brain, and miles of cable, wired into every building its central nervous system. There is very little in the Community to which the command post sentinels don't have access. *Walls have given way to wires. Privacy has given way to security. The Computer controls everything.* This is the embodiment of an Orwellian dream. But the scene *is* *not science fiction.* It is the Las Colinas housing development, Irving, Texas, September 1979. All of the technology for an almost totally electronic lifestyle is here and being installed *rapidly throughout the Dallas area.* And all of the moral and social questions raised by George Orwell's prophecies are facing us today.''

With all the data banks collected by the United States Government on each individual, would anyone question why the Chairman of the Senate Panel Probing United States Intelligence Agencies said recently,

''The government has the technological capacity to impose total tyranny if a dictator ever came to power, and there would be no place to hide.''

Another excerpt from an article entitled, ''When TV Sees You,'' Desmond Smith, a Producer for the Canadian Broadcasting Corporation says:

''The Era of one-way television dominated by three commercial networks and their seven hundred and twenty-five affiliated stations is ending. Soon, viewers will be able to 'talk back' to their television sets using two-way, computer-linked television delivered by cable. In New York, Atlanta, Pittsburgh, Chicago and Philadelphia, applications have been filed and in some instances already approved for citywide cable franchises. To broaden the financial base, such mega-sized cable systems can therefore be expected to expand rapidly into the transmission of non-television services. Two-way television systems pry into subscriber privacy by their ability to monitor user's choices continuously. As the new technology enters our homes, television usage will include our hitherto *private thoughts, habits and feelings.*

"At the present time there are absolutely no guarantees that subscribers of two-way television systems can be protected from abuse, either from inside or from wiretappers outside the systems. Unless the cable companies that are planning to introduce them or the city officials who seem so quick to approve two-way cable television can resolve this question of privacy, viewer beware may well be the prudent course to follow when the salesman arrives at the door. *The price of admission is computer surveillance.*"

CBS's Daniel Schorr, speculated about the invasion of privacy in an article datelined Aspen, Colorado, September 4, 1978, entitled "Communication Explosion Reverberates Throughout World," in which he stated:

"Much of the world seems to live in dread of being subjected to a universal Kojack."

## Fiber Optics

This system is made possible, and is currently being developed by the implementation of a tiny glass thread about the size of a human hair, called a fiber optic. It is eighty times lighter than previously used copper wire, and has a much larger information transfer capacity. Fiber optic systems are static proof; do not spark or short circuit, are resistant to electromagnetic disturbances, and are much less expensive to install.

This glass thread can transmit 500,000 bits of information per second; 100,000 different radio programs; or, 100 different telecasts; and 2,500 different telephone conversations simultaneously.

> "Few people know that this tiny fiber optic cable is a two-way light pipe; at the television end it will not only bring the signal into your home, but there are little pinhead sized *fish eye lenses in the cable which can watch you. They are visiting you in your living room without your knowledge.* The first 10,000 units were built and installed without anyone knowing it, because the lenses are built into the cable. These cables were installed under the *false premise* that this little lens would allow the set to adjust for different light levels in your room!" On the end, "a little *fish eye lens picks up everybody who is in the room where the television set is, **and the speaker is already two-way! This is a gross invasion of privacy. A person may be ten miles away in a television transmitting studio, but he can see* and *hear* everything in your television room" so states Dr. Patrick Fisher in *Eye of the Antichrist,* a Southwest Radio Church Publication.

He further reported the set will monitor whether *on or off* and that a computer could do the monitoring and store in its memory banks what it is programmed to pick out on a particular person.

For those of you who think that the fiber optic business is in its embryonic stages, Daniel Schorr indicates in his article, that fiber optics was a billion dollar a year industry in the United States already!

## "1984" Style Control

Thus, it becomes obvious that the Antichrist will seize this system of video-telephonic hookups to moniter the activities of each person on earth. If anyone refuses to take the prescribed number on the forehead or hand, there will be further inducements to conformity.

''A strange, artificial sound that can wipe the mind clean and turn people into obedient robots has been developed by British scientists. So highly dangerous is this sound that the master tape on which it is recorded has been locked up in an underground vault in London. Declared Dr. Robert Sharpe, a noted behavioral phychologist who helped develop it, 'This sound is dynamite. In the wrong hands the sound could be put to sinister uses. It would be possible for a government to *broadcast the sound, wiping people's minds clean.* Any propaganda could then be broadcast, and the people would believe it.' When we played the sound to volunteers through

earphones, the EEG machine showed their brains to be asleep — making them receptive to any information we chose to give them."
*National Enquirer,* October 5, 1976.

This will be a convenient tool to use on political opponents. After the sound is broadcast, these people will believe, and do anything they are instructed to do, becoming "programmed robots."

## Missing Persons?
### *Update 1982*

Some scientists have indicated that there were satellites circling the earth capable of emitting partial beams (lasers) with an accuracy of less than five feet. Surveillance by these satellites covered the entire world in 1980. More recently this technology advanced to an exact science with enemy lasers capable of destroying our missiles seconds after launch.

The Antichrist will wield the power not only to destroy enemy weapons which move with the speed of sound, but may also use this same technology to "clean up" the world environment from the arch enemies of this World Government. This *absolute totalitarian* will not have to worry about mercy killings as did Hitler, with clumsy removal of bodies, then burials; only a blob *who* will burn up in less than a minute.

## Worship via TV?

"And all that dwell upon the earth shall worship him, whose names are not written in the book of life." Revelation 13:8.

Nebuchadnezzar had his servants blow instruments of music at preannounced times, and all people everywhere had to fall down and worship the golden image. The Antichrist will simply require worship before the television screens at some specified time. The computers that monitor your televisions will receive transmissions back in their memory bank on just how often, and how gracious your worship is of this beast and his image.

## "His Image"

John heard the angel say, "If any man worship the beast and his image . . . " Revelation 14:9.

For centuries Bible scholars have conjectured various arrangements for this beast's image. More recently there have been suspicions that it would merely be a super-complex talking computer. Computers are now developed that can pick up words, translate, and speak them in every language. But, John said, "an image." On Donahue's NBC television program recently, there was an "Electronic Image" that appeared as a guest!

In the October 1980 issue of the magazine, *Discover,* dozens of pictures from still life to a portrait of a lady, are shown beautifully depicted (or drawn) with numbers in complex equations supplied by the International Information Computer. While these look like the work of an artist, there is no substance, only an image. Quoting from this article:

"In the computer world, these Renaissance men are called graphicists. They must convert the qualities that make an object look real — the transparency of a champagne glass, the

127

shadows of spoons on a table — into the algebraic and geometric formulas that define them. The computer can understand these formulas, *and can translate them into an image.*"

The article indicates that 72 million calculations were needed for the image shown on page 131. It further states that "this picture taxed the Information International Computer, but the firm hopes to convince Hollywood that scenes still created with props can be better done by Computer Graphics."

I conjecture that the Antichrist's image will thusly be depicted by graphicists from numerical equations derived from the root value of the number "6," and be transmitted via television around the world at "Worship Time."

Oh, John, you were more than a saint. You were a stickler for details, infinitesimally accurate!

## Mail by Computer

The United States Postal Service announced August 15, 1980, that an electronic service will be offered for delivering messages by computer. This will eliminate the heretofore privacy our letters enjoyed.

Washington (AP) in an article entitled "Electronic Mailing Planned" is stated:

"The service, the first system for delivering first-class mail without carrying paper from point to point, will go into effect January 4, 1982, the mail agency's governing board said.

128

The board expressed the hope that the Electronic Computer-Originated Mail service 'will be a milestone in the Postal Service's continuing effort to use computer and telecommunications advances to modernize the mails.' ''

Thus we see the Antichrist's power to control will be matched only by his ability and means.

**Computer "Images"**

129

# CHAPTER V

# THE AGE OF "6"

God created man on the sixth day. Genesis 1:27. God finished His work on the sixth day. Everything He had made was very good and the evening and morning were the sixth day. Genesis 1:31. He programmed man to amplify upon it for six days (thousand year days). II Peter 3:8.

Man's number in the Scripture is "6." The square of 6 is 36. The sum total of all numbers in this square, $1+2+3+4+5 \ldots +35+36=666$.

Man's most colossal work in the scriptures is epitomized by the number "6." Nebuchadnezzar, a King of Kings (Daniel 2:37), most typifies the highest and purest order of work yet accomplished by a man. His image was "66" cubits high and "6" cubits wide . . . a trinity of "6's." Daniel 3:1.

Archbishop Ussher of Armagh in 1650-1654 A.D., calculated the dates of important Biblical events and though much scholarly work has subsequently been done, the timetable remains virtually unchanged. Ussher calculated the date Adam and Eve were driven from the garden as 4,000 B.C. We are now almost 2,000 years A.D. It doesn't take a genius to see that God has allotted man 6,000 years to do his work and the seventh thousand-year period will be God's Sabbath, the Millennium Reign of the Government of Christ.

To condense this research into a brief synopsis, it appears obvious that man entered the age of "6," the age which will reflect the unparalleled excellence of both His work, and a man personally, in the twentieth century.

Epitomizing man's most excellent efforts of this century are two notable achievements: (1) The launching of the first reportedly unsinkable ocean going vessel, the Titanic. Named from the Greek word Titan, meaning gigantic, in Greek characters it has the numerical value of "666." (2) The landing of three men on the moon's surface in the decade of the 60's. A book entitled, *Prophecy Fulfilled In The Fateful Sixties,* reports that this was accomplished in an Apollo space flight:

- "Apollo has '6' letters.

- Each of the Astronaut's names has six letters:
  LOVELL    ANDERS    BORMAN
  6            6          6

- From space, '6' television transmissions were made.

- The moon trip was a '6' day journey.

- The spacecraft was in '6' sections.

131

- The Astronauts section plus the escape system was '66' feet tall.

- This Apollo flight grossed out at '6' million pounds.

- To escape earth's gravity, it had to achieve a velocity of '6' miles per second.

- Enroute time to the moon was '66' hours.

- The spacecraft entered the moon's gravitational field in the '6th' segment of the flight.

- The gravity of the moon is '1/6' of that on earth.

- The orbit around the moon was flown 66 miles above the moon's surface, at 6,000 mph.

- The Astronauts returned to earth on the '6th' day of the week.

- The capsule in which they returned weighed '6' tons.

- It had to be meticuously maneuvered to '6' degrees of the local horizon to reenter earth's atmosphere or bounce off into infinity.

- The helicopter which plucked the reentry capsule out of the water had a big '66' on its side.''

A more recent, yet equally momentous stride yet launching mankind into the age of ''6'' was taken June 5, 1975, when Anwar Sadat did a turn-about face, and officially reopened the Suez Canal after eight years to commercial navigation. He chose to do it with great pomp and ceremony in the Egyptian Destroyer

October "6," which bore the bold number on its bow "666." See *AP* Wire Photo.

Immediately after this date, the prefix "666" began to surface in economic news around the world. Reports began to be heard that the prefix for the forthcoming World Electronic Money System, (Cashless Society), would be "666."

Some IBM equipment that year began to bear the number "666" preceded by a date symbol. Howard Estep, *Prophetic Newsletter,* November 1975.

"At General Motor's headquarters in Detroit, they are talking about 1976 as a '6-6-6' year." August 1976, *The Jack Van Empe Crusade Newsletter.*

The movie industry, more abreast of the times than the Church, heralded 1976 with a "666" movie, *The Omen.* It depicted a World Dictator, possessed by Satan, Mr. "666" himself and the "mark of the beast" based on Revelation, chapter 13.

Concurrently, the European Common Market Trademark began to appear in shoes made in *Italy.* The trademark is a circle with a line drawn through the middle with a picture of a lamb on top with horns, and on the bottom half, the number "666," reports Dr. Michael Esses in his book, *The Next Visitor To Planet Earth.* See illustration.

"And I beheld another beast coming up out of the earth; and he had two horns like a lamb, and he spake as a dragon." Revelation 13:11.

The prefix was then observed on computer units made by Lear Siegler, Inc. with "LSI" in one circle and "666" in the other circle. See picture. (*Van Empe's Newsletter*, September 1975.) The number began to surface in so many places that at this point I refer you back to Chapter One for a more complete list of its usage worldwide.

And finally, we facetiously refer to man's most stupendous efforts at gambling, which ended much like the Titantic. On September 20, 1980, Associated Press reported *six* persons were indicted by a Pennsylvania grand jury for rigging the daily lottery drawing at WTAE-TV in Pittsburgh. "The result was a '666' winning number that paid a record $3.5 million."

## Will the Real Mr. "666" Please Stand?

Will there be "a man" whose name will numerically total the number "666"? Let us look at some major translation of Revelation 13:18.

"It is the number of *a man*, and *his number* is six hundred threescore and six." KJV

"The numerical values of the letters in his name add to '666.' " LB

"The number stands for a man's name. Its number is '666.' " TEV

"For it is *man's number*. His number is '666.' " NIV

"It is the number of a man, and its number is six hundred and sixty-six." RSV

"It is the number of a man. The number

'666.' '' Jerusalem Bible

"The number represents a man's name, and the numerical value of its letters is six hundred and sixty-six." NEB

Two of these translations state it is "man's number," "a human number," but, the others maintain dogmatically that it will be a man, the letters of whose name will numerically total "666."

Let us examine other necessary criteria:

## Place of Antichrist's Nativity

He must "come up among" the Ten Roman Empire nations. Daniel 7:8; 9:26. The Roman Empire extended South to the Sahara in Africa and did include Egypt.

The four great Empires which Daniel saw were analogized by four great beasts; the lion, representing Babylon; the bear, representing the Medo-Persian; the leopard, representing Greece, and the dreadful, terrible iron-teeth beast, the Roman Empire. Daniel 7. John uses these same beasts to indicate the territory that will make up the Antichrist's Kingdom. Revelation 13:1-2. While his kingdom will be the Western Powers, his influence will be world wide.

## Country

Syria, Daniel 11:28; Assyria, Micah 5:5; Nimrod's land, Micah 5:6; Chaldaea, Habakkuk 1:6; and Egypt, Jeremiah 46:7; which is plainly the Arab world.

*Aram* was "the name of Syria and of its people." Numbers 23:7. Mesopotamia is Aram-naharaim. Aram was thus a broad term designating the lands of the fertile crescent from Mesopotamia to Phoenicia. Its people came out of the same *Arabian* reservoir of Semitic peoples as the Hebrews and were closely related to Israel, with whom their history was intertwined, sometimes in alliance, often in conflict." *The Zondervan Pictorial Bible Dictionary.*

"A somewhat indefinite region bounded in general by the Taurus mountains, the Euphrates, the Syrian and Arabian deserts, Northern Palestine, and the Mediterranean. II Samuel 8:6, 15:8; Luke 2:2; Acts 15:23, 41. Its political history is interwoven with the *Assyrian, Babylonian, Persian, Greek, Roman,* and *Mohammedan* Empires." *Bible Encyclopedia Index Concordance and Dictionary,* Gilbert James Brett, Editor.

"Assyria was taken over in the third millenium B.C." by *Semites* from Arabia.

"The last quarter of the Seventh Century B.C. saw its subjugation by the Chaldean conquerors of Babylonia." *Zondervan Pictorial Bible Dictionary.*

In summation, we see his background is Semitic and Aramitic. He is a descendant of Abraham, but not a Jew.

## Religion: *Islam*

"He will have no regard for the *gods* of his fathers, nor for the god beloved of women." Daniel 11:37 LB

"He will show no regard for the *gods* of his fathers or for the one desired by women." NIV

"He will ignore his ancestral *gods,* and the god beloved of women." NEB

All translations from the most ancient manuscripts indicate:

1. His ancestors worshiped many *gods, plural*! They were polytheistic! Egyptians once worshiped many gods, but now are Moslems.

2. He would be expected to worship Tammuz! This is the Babylonian god that is placed in the Temple when it is desecrated in mid-week by the Antichrist. Ezekiel 8:14.

This verse as translated, in the King James Version says, "Neither shall he regard the God of his fathers, nor the desire of women." There have been those who have speculated that he would be a sexual pervert. Sorry, it has nothing to do with his sexuality. This refers to a god women especially desire.

## Diplomacy: *Detente*

"Peace, Peace,"

"Peace and Safety."

"*He shall come in peaceably . . .*" Daniel 11:21.

"*He shall enter peaceably;*" Daniel 11:21;24.

These peaceful gestures will continue for the first-three and one-half years, then wars will begin.

(Please keep in mind that the Antichrist will represent the temporal power, while the False Prophet will head up the ecclesiastic. The ecclesiastic will be in ascendancy the first 1260 days only to be destroyed in Midweek.)

### President Sadat, Egypt, and "666"

I have said of President Anwar Sadat: *"The number he chose on the warship he rode was an omen of things to come."*

Never have I spoken truer words. The NAME of the warship he rode, "OCTOBER 6," on that historic day in 1975 omniously predicted the date of his assassination.

Indeed, it was after he rode the warship #666, that 6 years later on October 6, 6 of his countrymen would take his life. Later his *"procession was borne along October Sixth Avenue named for the October 6, 1973 Egyptian offensive that opened the last Arab-Israeli war."* Cairo (AP) 10/10/81.

**I maintain Sadat is History's nearest prototype of the Jewish False Messiah!** Few events in history equal the prophetic significance of Sadat's aligning Egypt with Israel, and thus engineering the Middle East Policy which sets the stage for Daniel's 70th week. If we are close enough to the end of the age, Egypt will continue *"in league"* with Israel for Egypt is conspicuously missing in the nations which attack Israel in Ezekiel 38, though historically Egypt has been Israel's most consistent foe. Furthermore, Egypt will become a dumping ground for the Jews dur-

138

ing Jacob's Trouble, appearing to be their friend, but will turn on the Jews (when great numbers are settled there, Isaiah 19:18-20), at the time of the very end and attempt to exterminate them. It is because of this deceit and abuse, Egypt will be cursed 40 years. Exodus 29:9-15. I hold to these things: Sadat was the Prime Mover and Chief Architect of this end-time deception of the Jews. And, since he reversed his war policy against Israel, and reopened the Suez Canal in 1975, he has *"conspicuously identified"* with this number "666."

Keep your eyes on Egypt, and its leader. This trap of deceit is set. The end time *"fierce King"* of Egypt, (Isaiah 19:4) who will have deceived the Jews into believing he is their friend, will wreak havoc on them during Jacob's Trouble. One day this deception will consummate in the embodiment of Deceit, the False Messiah, Mr. 666.

The other side of the coin. Israel's chief contributor to the "Peace Plan" with Egypt, Moshe Dayan, died 10 days later on October 16, 1981. He was 66. It appears obvious to me that this plan to surrender large parts of land of Israel to Egypt is not pleasing to God. Everytime Israel has been attacked, her borders have been enlarged . . . by God.

Remember that those who get the victory over the Antichrist (the False Messiah) will not sing a new song; (as the elders in Revelation 5:9), but *"The Song of Moses."* Revelation 15:2-3. This song is identified as Exodus 15, where Moses is singing about victory over Pharaoh — the first to enslave Israel. Another Pharaoh will obviously be the last to enslave Israel.

Port Said, June 5, 1975 (AP) "Surrounded by a swarm of small craft, the Egyptian Navy Destroyer 'October 6,' with President Sadat aboard, enters the Suez Canal at Port Said and thus re-opens the canal for commercial shipping. . ." (AP Wirephoto) On the bow was the number 666.

# CHAPTER VI

*"This King will make a Seven-Year Treaty with the people (Israel)."*
Daniel 27 LB.

# THE SEVEN-YEAR TREATY

JERUSALEM *(AP)* 6-16-80 — ''The Israeli Cabinet rejected the European Common Market Nations' offer to guarantee Israel's security . . .''

I opened the morning newspaper and read this remarkable account of the EEC's offer to guarantee Israel's security. I mused aloud, ''This is incredible!'' This Monday in Montgomery, Alabama, I am reading about the negotiations of the treaty which Israel scoffed at today, but presently, will accept when made by the Charismatic Leader to arise out of the European (Roman Empire) Nations. Then the somber countdown will officially begin for the last Seven Years of this World Order. With staid excitement I arose and climbed the stairs into my study, and opened the only book that is more current than the newspaper. I read Daniel 9:27. Me thinks . . . it makes Daniel's 70th week appear very, very near. Significantly, there are many contemporaries, men of some stature, who obviously agree with the assessment. Some are boldly declaring that the last generation began in 1948, and that the end of this age will occur around 1988.

In addition, some of these are indicating that they believe Russia will move against Israel very soon, and that this battle will start the countdown for the last seven years.

It is at this point I believe many sincere Bible students confuse things that differ. *Before Russia marches on Israel, this treaty, now in its embryonic form, must be enacted to guarantee Israel's security for this last Seven-Year period. How else could* Ezekiel 38:8, 11, and 14 be possible? These indicate that Israel MUST BE AT REST AND DWELLING SAFELY . . . a far cry from their precarious posture now. The only way Israel can possibly attain this "rest and safety" is accepting the protection of this very treaty. Not only will they be safe, they will be prospering greatly, under the protection of this treaty.

Israelis now pay 60% income tax to support in large part their defense programs. This need for exorbitant taxation will be eliminated when they no longer need to build their defenses, and these revenues will then go into private enterprise. The evil thought that Russia will think (38:10) is that Israel will be the only nation in the world not under Socialism (see next chapter), and they will be accumulating riches — so much so, that Russia will desire to take from them a spoil: gold, silver, cattle, and goods. Ezekiel 38:13. The Russians have prophetically commemorated the battle with a 14-kopek postage stamp issued in 1930. See illustration.

**Above: A copy of the 14 kopek Russian stamp which commemorates their coming invasion with Israel, admitting their identity as the Gog and Magog of Ezekiel chapter 38. Courtesy of *Christ For The Nations,* February 1980, Volume 32, Number 11.**

I therefore strongly believe that Russia will not attack Israel until after the rise of the Antichrist; the negotiation of this treaty by the Europeans, and the acceptance of this security by the Israelis. Russia must make this move against Israel in the initial phase of the latter half of this Seven-Year period, Jacob's Trouble. The first three and one-half years for Israel will be in ''peace and safety,'' and prosperity. I further see Israel yielding all its nuclear weapons in exchange for this protection, becoming so vulnerable to attack that God has to effect a ''Sodom-Gomorrah'' type defeat on Russia; thus magnifying Himself and making sure He is known in the eyes of many nations as ''The Lord.'' Ezekiel 38:22-23. I see a continuing series of battles right up to the Armageddon, closing the Seven-Year Period and the Age.

CHAPTER VII

*Wars and rumors of wars, see that*
*ye be not troubled.*

JESUS CHRIST 33 AD

# WORLD WAR III

Where does World War III fit into Daniel's 70th week, the last seven years of this world age? It doesn't. I see World War III as the necessary conflagration that will precede this week and produce a world state of Socialism; reduce everyone to a number where computers will determine one's allowance in an international ration system.

I remember the sober expression on the face of Dr. Billy Graham as he concluded his television Christmas message of 1979 with these words:

> "We are poised on the brink of disaster. Our everyday headlines seem to suggest that our world is hurtling out of control. We are on the very verge of Armageddon . . . Wake up, America, wake up."

We differed only in semantics. We are on the verge of World War III to be followed in quick succession by the rise of the World Dictator; the negotation of the Seven-Year Peace Treaty with Israel, and three and one-half years later, Russia's march on Israel; then Armageddon at the close of this Seven-Year period.

Only a few days later, I listened to the assessment of Pope John Paul II, who related, ''Somewhere, someday, someone, somehow will press the button and the world will experience nuclear holocaust, and this concerns me; but it is the astronomical overkill that is particularly disturbing.''

One hydrogen bomb encased in cobalt has the capacity to annihilate three of the 4.5 billion people living on the earth. In January 1980, there were fifty thousand of these nuclear weapons in the world, controlled by several different nations. In March 1980, the United States Government awarded a contract to Boeing Aircraft to build another three thousand cruise nuclear missiles, and if Salt II is not signed, the number will be increased to ten thousand.

On the heels of this, Governor Jerry Brown lamented:

''We are headed for World War III probably preceded by a world depression. Currently, the United States is an island of affluence in a sinking sea of despair without any hope.''

March 21, 1980, the President of France complained:

''The world is unhappy because it doesn't know where it is going, and it fears that if it knew, it would be headed toward disaster . . . it fears impending holocaust.''

I thought of the names of men who are very politically astute, as Mr. Kissinger, Alexander Solzhenitzyn, Britain's Lord Home, Chinese Premier Chou En-lai and others who have stated that "the early years of the decade of the 1980's will be years of maximum international peril." WAR IN EARLY 1980's? *Omega Generation Update.*

And for what it's worth, an *AP* writer from the *Vatican* wrote (10-13-78), of a *Twelfth Century* prophecy by Saint Malachy, who wrote mottos for each succeeding Pope. Predicted for the 264th Pope (Pope John Paul II), the text is quoted as saying:

> "A great punishment will fall upon mankind in the second half of the Twentieth Century . . . Satan will succeed in seducing the spirits of the great scientists who invent the arms with which it will be possible to destroy a large part of mankind in a few minutes. A great war will be unleashed in the second half of the Twentieth Century. Millions and millions of men will envy the dead."

Not only did he predict the calamity to occur during the reign of the 264th Pope, but he predicted it to occur during the latter half of the Twentieth Century. His prophecies extend to only one more Pope!

Then there is the book which occupies the spot under the Bible on President Carter's desk in the Oval Office. *The Third World War,* by John Hackett, who assesses the world militarily, historically, and contemporarily, and sets the date of World War III in August, 1985.

Unlike several sincere colleagues, I predict that Russia will make her next move not against oil-less Israel, but to seize the oil of the Middle East; thus paralyzing Western Europe's economy in an estimated thirty days, and sufficiently restricting the military capability of the United States, so that she can counter with only token force.

International Peace Research Commission predicted on its Tenth Anniversay an Atomic War in 1985. Willard Cantelon, *New Money Or None.*

January 1980, "Special Office Brief," Margaret Thatcher, Prime Minister of England:

"The Western Powers have wholly miscalculated the oil position. We feel our imperative duty to warn you that *within three years a gigantic crisis will occur.* At present, we have not even thought it out, let alone prepared a defense ability, be it military or moral. The dangers ahead vastly exceed those of 1914 or 1939. Indeed, the dangers are not even comparable." Reprinted in January 1980, *Midnight Cry.*

Other Europeans are expressing grave concern.

"Across Western Europe the conviction is growing that things are slipping so disastrously out of control, that World War III may be imminent . . . One analyst put it, 'The only way of keeping President Carter from doing something calamitous is to go along with his preliminary arrangements for Armageddon.' " *AP,* 4-25-80.

## U.S. CAN'T WIN A WAR, February 4, 1980:

*New York (AP)* "Dr. Edward Teller, known as the father of the hydrogen bomb, said the Soviet Union would win a nuclear exchange with the United States and that the United States would be destroyed. If we went into a nuclear war today, there is practically no question that the Russians would win that war and the United States would cease to exist, Teller said."

Not only do the Russians have superior nuclear capability, but they have forged dramatically ahead in the testing and production of the more potent Partial Beam Weapons, which allow the Soviets to intercept anything in the air before it strikes Russian soil.

"The Soviet Union has achieved a technical breakthrough in high energy physic application that may soon provide it with a directed energy beam weapon capable of *neutralizing* the entire United States Ballistic Missile Force. The hard proof of eight successful Soviet tests of directed energy beam technology give new and overriding urgency to bring these developments into the public domain . . . and rip the veil of intelligence secrecy, a matter of survival." *Aviation Week & Space Technology*, June 2, 1977.

"The Soviets already have tested a Buck-Rogers-type death ray particle beam." *UPI*, Washington, D.C.

Now, our Defense Secretary, Harold Brown, admits in a speech delivered at the Naval War College at Newport, Rhode Island, August 20, 1980, and carried by *Associated Press,* that:

"Russia's missile force . . . may already be able to threaten destruction of United States land based missiles."

Another article of grave concern is entitled, *"There Is A Nuclear Weapon In Your Back Yard,"* by Dr. Peter Beter, in which he states:

"The Soviet weapons in our coastal waters are a very grave danger to American Security, so says Dr. Peter Beter. The missiles planted so far, are ready to fire . . . lurking in our own territorial waters ready for underwater launch upon satellite command. They are also in the waters of thirty countries worldwide, Dr. Beter says that ninety-six underwater missiles were planted in American waters and were still there January 15, 1977." *Midnight Cry,* June 1977.

*U.S. News and World Report,* November 12, 1979, sums it up well:

"Fifteen years of miscalculations about Russian military intentions now are catching up with the United States. That is the conclusion of top defense analysts."

I listened intently to a top military official who declared that laser weapons (partial beam), obsolete everything in our military arsenals; and, another who recently declared that every American city could be destroyed in seventeen minutes just from Russia's present nuclear capability.

I remember my Chemistry Professor explained to me in the 1960's that at that time they didn't teach the mechanics of lasers for fear it would fall into the hands of a distorted person. He continued,

> "A laser beam aimed at an airliner would melt everything in the scope of its beam including the atmospheric elements, the sides of the airliner and the part of the passengers bodies that were within the scope of the rays; all soundless, sightless, and odorless."

The truth is, the mechanics of lasers were taught, and the technology applied in many beneficial areas; but, distorted minds are still around.

In the *Detroit News,* August 10, 1979, was an article which indicated that Westland Council, suburb of Detroit, had approved a cable television system that among other things made *stray dogs* disappear! The disappearance (melting) of stray dogs did not strike fear in my heart; but, the same capability could cause the disappearance of the senile, the handicapped, the elderly; reminiscent of World War II, when Hitler "tidied up" Germany's society with far less sophisticated means: mercy killings and buryings. There'll be no burials needed for those whose bodies are melted by death rays from *already orbiting satellites.*

While I hope and pray that Russia will not win World War III, the end-time scenario calls for a loose federation of Socialist states as a necessary posture for the final formation and implementation of the One World Government. This Socialist Regime, which may come about from as much compromise as combat, will then require the Number long before assigned to people of the world on plastic cards to now be marked on the forehead or hand in exchange for which each person will be doled out their day's rations; ''a loaf of bread (or a quart of wheat) for a day's wages.'' Revelation 6:6.

There is massive unrest in the Communist nations. The first strike occurred in Russia, followed by massive strikes in Poland, in the Summer of 1980. The chief complaint — insufficient bread and meat. These are not signs about which the Western World should cheer. They are ominous rumblings of domestic deterioration which have historically been dealt with by forging an issue of greater unrest to the surface, around which the nation can rally . . . the issue is invariably war.

Ultra Orthodox Jewish Rabbi Shabatai Shiloh, and other Rabbis in Israel have asserted recently that there will be three great wars ending this age. The solemn sequence will, in my opinion be:

1. World War III (the next catastrophe), from which the world will emerge with a world-wide Socialist Federation of Nations, maintaining some semblance of national identity to the very end. Daniel 11:41.

Whoever is triumphant in World War III, will be devoid of a diplomat who can achieve an effective liaison with Israel. (Israel will be like a thorn in the side of the world, "a burdensome stone.") "Jerusalem will be a heavy stone burdening the world." Zechariah 12:3. All the world will be made to believe that there could be international peace if it were not for the Jews.

This is the posture of the world that will lend itself to the rise of a World Dictator, (not in line for royal succession, Daniel 11:21) and without military force, he will solidly unite Western Europe coming from among the Ten Nation Federation. Even Russia will succumb to his flattery and intrigue and yield to his leadership abilities. His greatest virtue will be that he will convince the Jews that he is their Messiah, offer a treaty of protection for seven years, and at last the world will cry, PEACE AND SAFETY. (I Thessalonians 5:3). This will last in varying degrees about three and one-half years.

The Jews will relax, and enter an unparalleled period of prosperity. Israel will be the only nation in the world still engaged in private enterprise, of which Russia in particular will become jealous. Though the world will be a Federation of Socialist States, there will still be a King of the North, of the South, and of the East, during the reign of West Europe's Dictator (The "Other Christ"). Daniel 11.

2. Russia invades Israel; after three and one-half years of peace and safety, Russia will become enraged at Israel's prosperity; think an evil thought and come to take a spoil.

3. Armageddon; closing out the seven years, all nations will gather against Jerusalem (Jeremiah 25); and "the slain of the Lord will be from one end of the

152

earth to the other end.''

What happens to the oil after the final battle of World War III remains a mystery. Possibly, it might be depleted. The wells could be blown up in the ensuing takeover. But, the battle of Ezekiel 38, when Russia and her allies march on Israel, is conspicuously devoid of oil. ''All of them will come out of the North parts riding horses (Ezekiel 38:15), and combat will be man to man (38:4), *all* of them handling swords.'' Russia's war with Israel may not be nuclear and appears to be reduced to an attack by cavalrymen.

Surely, ''men's hearts shall be failing them for fear''; but take heart, the Christian is specifically excluded from those who will be overtaken by fear.

''Ye shall hear of wars and rumors of wars''; but in this same breath and sentence we read, ''see that ye be not troubled,'' Matthew 24:6. ''Let not *your* heart be troubled neither let it be afraid,'' John 14:27. ''The fearful and unbelieving shall have their part in the lake of fire,'' Revelation 21:8.

Thank you, Father, for keeping us in perfect peace whose mind is stayed on you!

*This book is published by:*

Ministries, Inc.
Post Office Box 4038
Montgomery, Alabama 36104 (205) 262-4891

CHAPTER VIII

# THE GREAT
# PROPHETIC EVENT
# THAT SIGNALS THE END

In November 1979, a Southern Baptist Seminary graduate spoke to a packed out assembly in north Alabama (and subsequently in many places), that he had been instructed by the Holy Spirit to inform the Church that she had ''now entered the Great Tribulation period.''

In June 1980, I received a call from a young evangelist who exclaimed, ''Sister, didn't you know that we have been in the Great Tribulation since 1967?''

A few days ago, a lady in some distress phoned me and said, ''I had been taught that Christians would be 'taken out' before the development of the One World Government and the 'revealing of the Antichrist.' Now, Dr. Pat Robertson and others are teaching that we may go through the entire seven-year period. Can you explain to me simply without alluding to whether or not the Church will be here, how I can know when the world enters Daniel's 70th week (the last seven years of this World Order)?'' I replied humbly, that I would make an attempt. This chapter is an amplification of that effort.

There is one astoundingly recognizable event which must occur at the onset that will portend or foreshadow; signal and indicate the *beginning* of these last seven years:

## The Revealing of the Antichrist (Other Christ)

"Be not soon shaken in mind, or be troubled, neither by spirit, nor by word, nor by letter as from us, as that the day of Christ is at hand. Let no man deceive you by any means: for that day shall not come, except there come a falling away first, and that man of sin be revealed, the son of perdition; . . . For the mystery of iniquity doth already work: only he who now letteth will let, until he be taken out of the way. And then shall that Wicked (One) be revealed . . ." II Thessalonians 2:2-8.

"The most learned and exhaustive interpretations of the events during the time immediately preceding and following the coming of the Lord is done by Elliot in his four volumes entitled, *Horae Apolypticae.* Volume 1:65 holds that Antichrist means another Christ, a *pro-*Christ, a *vice*-Christ, a pretender to the name of Christ, *and in that character,* an usurper and adversary." *Systematic Theology,* Augustus H. Strong, P1006.

The greatest misconception **spawned** by Satan now

155

reverberating throughout Christendom is that this World Leader will be catapulted to center stage using a long forked tongue, with blood dripping from his spiny fingers, the embodiment of all that is cruel, heartless, and sinister; immediately deploying military force, "plucking up three of the Ten European Nations," and in general, sending blood curdling chills up the spine of the inhabitants of the world!

Oh, how unfortunate to be so deceived. Jesus said, "Take heed that no man deceive you." Matthew 24:4. Paul cried, "Let no man deceive you BY ANY MEANS."

The chief activity of Satan is not murder, fornication, etc. These are results of his primary activity, which is deception. When Satan is bound for a thousand years, it is his power to deceive that is abolished, but all other sins cease. When he is loosed again, he shall go out to "deceive" again. Revelation 20:3&8.

This World Dictator will be the consummation of Satan's grandest efforts to deceive mankind; a skilled Charlatan masquerading as the "Anointed of God," the "False Christ"; the "Other Messiah." This person will be history's greatest *emulator* of Jesus Christ. How else could he be mistaken as the "Anointed of God," the "False Messiah," the "Other Christ"?

- Jesus came into the world without pomp and ceremony. Although Christians know that He came from the "Ivory Palaces," the world construes his background (the stable, the carpenter's shop) as one of obscurity. Likewise, the Antichrist will be born in inconspicuousness.

156

- Jesus' life was spent among the poor. "Foxes have holes, birds have their nests, but the Son of man hath not where to lay His head." His attention was rarely diverted to the wealthy and noble. "Go tell that fox," he once said of Herod. Likewise, the Antichrist will make his debut moving among the poor, the neglected, a Mahatma Ghandi type; the least suspected candidate in a list of many to become the "Other Christ."

- Christ was supernaturally empowered by the Holy Spirit being given to Him, "without measure" at a particular time and place; His baptism at Jordan; Luke 3:22, when God was ready for His ministry to begin. Likewise, this World Dictator will be supernaturally empowered at some specific time and place, even as "after the sop Satan entered into Judas; John 13:27, by Satan giving Antichrist the power with which to do his work.

- As Christ died on the cross, betrayed by His own, likewise the Antichrist will die, betrayed by one who ate at "his table." Daniel 11:26.

- As Jesus was resurrected by the power of the Holy Spirit, this World Dictator will be resurrected from the bottomless pit by the power of Satan. The Satanic incarnation (empowering) will come at the time he ascends from the bottomless pit; "power was given to him to continue 42 months." Revelation 13:5; 17:8.

This World Dictator will rise out of obscurity moving in and out of the poor masses of the world. Ultimately, he will succeed in his role as "emulator of the Anointed of God." His super deceit will convince the Jews that he is their long awaited Messiah. Additionally, the whole world will wonder at and worship him. Revelation 13:3-4.

## His Rise

"He shall *come* in peaceably." Daniel 11:21.

"He shall *enter* peaceably." Daniel 11:24.

This World Leader will set precedents in every endeavor including his entrance. He will be the first person in history to put a Kingdom together in the absence of the use of force. His greatest virtue will be his charismatic ability to espouse and implement peaceful gestures. The world will be so weary of war that he will be astutely careful to avoid even a hostile innuendo.

"Next to come to power will be an evil man not directly in line for royal succession. But, during a crisis he will take over the kingdom by flattery and intrigue. Then all opposition will be swept away before him, including a leader of the priests. His promises will be worthless. *From the first his method will be deceit; with a mere handful of followers,* he will become strong. He will enter the richest areas of the land without warning and do something never done before; *he will take the property and wealth of the rich and scatter it out among the people.*" Daniel 11:21-24. LB

This World Leader will emerge from anonymity with a handful of followers. He will dispel his lack of popularity with a massive deployment of the age-old gimmick of giving "something for nothing" to the poor; except this guy goes overboard with it. He sets another precedent by literally taking it from the rich, and giving it to the poor in one action. It works like magic! Suddenly, the poor masses are at his steps. Having clinched his rise by becoming the Twentieth Century Robin Hood, he turns his charm and intrigue on the leaders of the European Kingdom. "Peace, Peace." "Peace and Safety." He gains posture with them by "speaking great things!" The world has been devoid of positive leadership for so long that they succumb to his unequivocal orations. These sound like beautifully orchestrated symphonies in the ears of these distraught politicians:

> "The world can have peace without war; an agriculture that is plentiful and prosperous; bustling commerce restored; an expanding and profitable industry; benevolence between management and labor; a renaissance in arts and letters, and poverty wiped from the face of the earth!"

Thus we shall sadly witness the rise of the Eighth World effort to govern mankind in peace. Revelation 17:10. Oh how sad that the world must learn again in this seven-year regime that Thomas Paine was right when he declared:

> "Government in its best state is but a necessary evil; in its worst state, an intolerable one."

# The Coalition, the Poor and the Rich

The decade of the 1980's began with two-thirds of the 4.5 billion inhabitants of the world having median incomes of less than $300 per year; the remaining one-third having median incomes in excess of $3,000. This "disparity" will be eliminated when this World Dictator assumes control, and "equitably" distributes the wealth of the world!

A very unlikely coalition endorsing this World Leader will be formed between the poor masses who will heartily approve of his efforts, and the very wealthy Apostate Church. Precursors of this coalition are already being heard, as ecumenical leaders are repeatedly calling on the wealthy to share their wealth with the poor.

## Ecumenism

An event of equal importance initiating the last seven years of this world order is the formation and implementation of the One World Apostate Church. This powerful and wealthy institution will incorporate into it the liberal elements of all faiths. This is the subject of a forthcoming publication by the author which will link this One World Apostate Church to the "666 System," even as the thrust of this book is to expose the economic and political structures of the world in the "666 System."

This One World Apostate Church headed up by its False Prophet will represent the ecclesiastic arm of the One World Government, and it will be this institution which will promote the political leader and finally announce to the world that the ''Other Christ'' is come. This False Prophet, not the Antichrist, does all the miracles. See Revelation 13. This ''apostasia'' (II Thessalonians 2:3) religious apostasy, is gaining momentum rapidly through the various ecumenical efforts. This must occur first for the man of sin to be revealed, who will negotiate this seven-year treaty with Israel, and start the countdown of this final seven-year period.

Most people would be shocked if they knew how deeply the world is already entrenched in Ecumenism! The father of the World Council of Churches, William Visser T. Hooft, said in the *Daily Oklahoman:*

> ''The international ecumenical movement has reached a point where its mission should be more one of stimulating dialogue among the world's religions *rather* than trying to win the entire world to Christ.''

When one reads about the activities of the World Council of Churches, and their support of the African Frelimo guerilla movement which now has an inmate population of over 100,000 in their concentration camps, many thousands of these dedicated Christians, and a huge list of Marxists whom the World Council of Churches has financially supported; it becomes obvious that their goal is Socialism, often called a more respectable term Humanism, which is working to bring about a One World Society, including, a One World Church.

George Cornell, *AP* Religion Writer, wrote an article in the *Hickory Daily Record,* entitled: "Religions Unite In Plea, It Is Not A Utopian Dream," September 9, 1979, Princeton, New Jersey.

"Humanity's great religions which sometimes railed or warred against each other in the past, have joined in a plea for a fair, neighborly world with no more war . . . but, the 337 Representatives of ten major historic faiths; Christian, Buddhist, Confucianist, Jewish, Jainist, Moslem, Sikh, Shintoist and Zorastrian agree that things now look frightening. 'We are approaching . . . a turning point in human history at which the survival of world civilization is at stake!' they said in a joint declaration at the close September 7, of a week long meeting at Princeton Theological Seminary.

"The 'Princeton Declaration' cited modern afflictions; the nuclear arms buildup, economic imbalances and exploitation, shrinking resources and crushing of human rights. But, it also proclaimed,

" 'We believe there is an alternative to violence; we believe that peace is possible . . . That all religions will increasingly cooperate in creating a responsible world community.'

" '*It was a truly religious United Nations,*' said the Rev. Homer A. Jack, the conference general secretary. He said, 'Never before has such a varied religious group met in such a harmonious atmosphere.'

162

*"Roman Catholic Archbishop Angelo Fernandez of New Delhi, was re-elected President of the World Conference on Religion and Peace,* founded ten years ago. It held previous assemblies in 1970 in Japan and 1974 in Belgium.

"The United States meeting was the first in this country, and it saw harsh dangers on the world's horizons; assaults on human dignity, the menace of nuclear weapons, technological and economic exploitation of the poor, political repression of dissidents, and environmental abuses.

"The conference pledged a 'global moral and religious campaign *which will say no to any kind of war* between nations or peoples.' "

Already all peoples of the world are sensing a need for a divinely appointed person to save them from war, extinction, and poverty. Islam is expecting a coming "Mahdi." Judaism is expecting a coming "Messiah." Christianity is expecting the "Messiah" to return.

Ecumenism is conditioning the world for the acceptance of the False Messiah, the Other Christ.

## Latin Language and "666"

Only six basic letters in Original Latin represented numbers; which differs from the Greek, Aramaic, Hebrew, Chaldee, etc., which utilized most-to-all of their characters. The six basic characters are:

I = 1, V = 5, X = 10, L = 50, C = 100, D = 500;
their sum total "666."

## Types of Antichrist and "666"

You might want to figure these out from the Alphabets and their numerical values at the end of this chapter. I have discovered four historical types of Antichrist: (1) Nimrod, (2) Antiochus IV, (3) Nero Caesar, and (4) Nebuchadnezzar, discussed earlier. We shall look at the first three:

(1) *Nimrod;* the first type of Antichrist, whose birthday was celebrated in ancient Rome (Saturnalia), December 25. In Chaldee, native language of Nimrod, Saturn is spelled STUR.

S =    60
T =    400
U =    6
R =    200
"666"

(2) *Antiochus IV,* a Syrian, in his attempt to hellenize the Jews, had a pig sacrificed on the altar in Jerusalem. He forbade circumcision and destroyed all Old Testament books he could find; placed an idol of Zeus (Jupiter) in the Holy of Holies and took for himself the official title "God Manifest," a term in Greek, called EPIPHANEIA. It has the numerical value of "666."

(3) *Caesar Nero:* From the time of the early Church Fathers, theologians have been divulging to us

the numerical value of his name in Hebrew. NRON KRS has the numerical value of "666."

N =      50
R =     200
O =       6
N =      50
K =     100
R =     200
S =      60
        ―――――
       "666"

Nero was best known for his severe persecutions of Christians. He turned them into human torches to light his gardens at night. He fed them to hungry lions for entertainment. He had them run through with swords. He burned them at the stakes in public ceremonies. It is officially estimated that the number of Christians buried in the catacombs of Rome is four million. These died at the hands of Nero, and subsequent Roman Emperors, the first three centuries after Christ. The "tribulation" was so widespread, Paul alluded to it in I Thessalonians 3:3,4.

> "That no man should be moved by these afflictions: for yourselves know that we are appointed thereunto. For verily, when we were with you, we told you before that we should suffer tribulation; even as it came to pass, and ye know."

This Antichrist to come will "make war with the saints and overcome them," much like Nero. Revelation 13:7 and Daniel 7:21.

Greek:

| | | | | |
|---|---|---|---|---|
| 1 | $A$ | $a$ | alpha | a |
| 2 | $B$ | $\beta$ | beta | b |
| 3 | $\Gamma$ | $\gamma$ | gamma | g |
| 4 | $\Delta$ | $\delta$ | delta | d |
| 5 | $E$ | $\epsilon$ | epsilon | e (short) |
| 6 | $Z$ | $\zeta$ | zeta | z (= dz) |
| 7 | $H$ | $\eta$ | eta | e (long) |
| 8 | $\Theta$ | $\theta$ | theta | th |
| 10 | $I$ | $\iota$ | iota | i |
| 20 | $K$ | $\kappa$ | kappa | k |
| 30 | $\Lambda$ | $\lambda$ | lambda | l |
| 40 | $M$ | $\mu$ | mu | m |
| 50 | $N$ | $\nu$ | nu | n |
| 60 | $\Xi$ | $\xi$ | xi | x |
| 70 | $O$ | $o$ | omicron | o (short) |
| 80 | $\Pi$ | $\pi$ | pi | p |
| 100 | $P$ | $\rho$ | rho | r |
| 200 | $\Sigma$ | $\sigma$ or $\varsigma$ | sigma | s |
| 300 | $T$ | $\tau$ | tau | t |
| 400 | $Y$ | $\upsilon$ | upsilon | u |
| 500 | $\Phi$ | $\phi$ | phi | ph |
| 600 | $X$ | $\chi$ | chi | ch |
| 700 | $\Psi$ | $\psi$ | psi | ps |
| 800 | $\Omega$ | $\omega$ | omega | o (long) |

Chaldee:

| | | | |
|---|---|---|---|
| 6 | U | 200 | R |
| 60 | S | 400 | T |

Many of the computations on the numerical values of the names and titles in this chapter were taken from the book *The Two Babylons*, by Alexander Hislop; and, Makluth Corporation, Box 012951, Miami, Florida 33101.

# Hebrew:

| | | | |
|---|---|---|---|
| 1. | א | 'Aleph (aw'-lef) | ' unappreciable |
| 2. | ב | Bêyth (bayth) | b |
| 3. | ג | Gîymel (ghee'-mel) | g hard = γ |
| 4. | ד | Dâleth (daw'-leth) | d [cent |
| 5. | ה | Hê' (hay) | h, often quies- |
| 6. | ו | Vâv (vawv) | v, or w quies- |
| 7. | ז | Zayin (zah'-yin) | z, as in zeal [cent |
| 8. | ח | Chêyth (khayth) | German ch = χ [(nearly kh) |
| 9. | ט | Têyth (tayth) | t = ת [cent |
| 10. | י | Yôwd (yode) | y, often quies- |
| 20 | ב, final ך | Kaph (caf) | k = ק |
| 30 | ל | Lâmed (law'-med) | l |
| 40 | מ, final ם | Mêm (mame) | m |
| 50 | נ, final ן | Nûwn (noon) | n |
| 60 | ס | Çâmek (saw'-mek) | ç = s sharp = שׂ |
| 70 | ע | 'Ayin (ah'-yin) | ' peculiar ' |
| 80 { | פ, final ף | Phê' (fay) | ph = f = φ |
| | פ | Pê' (pay) | p |
| 90 | צ, final ץ | Tsâdêy (tsaw-day') | ts |
| 100 | ק | Qôwph (cofe) | q = k = ק |
| 200 | ר | Rêysh (raysh) | r |
| 300 { | שׂ | Sîyn (seen) | s sharp = ס = s |
| | שׁ | Shîyn (sheen) | sh |
| 400 { | ת | Thâv (thawv) | th, as in thin |
| | ת | Tâv (tawv) | t = ט = t [= θ |

# Latin:

| 1 | I | |
|---|---|---|
| 5 | V | (also U when printed) |
| 10 | X | |
| 50 | L | |
| 100 | C | |
| 500 | D | |

The "M" has now come to be used also as a Roman numeral representing 1000. But originally, 1000 was written as CI with another C turned around, that is, CIↃ. This was later simplified into ⋒, and finally as M. See *Number in Scripture* by E.W. Bullinger, page 284.

"The predictions concerning Antichrist may have had a partial fulfillment in Antiochus Epiphanes, in Nero and Pagan Rome, and in the Papacy." Hodge, *Systematic Theology,* page 880.

## English Language, Antichrist, and "666"

Perhaps it is wise to place less than equal emphasis on the results of assigning numerical values to the English alphabet, since this language has historically been alphabetic. Unlike the more ancient alphabets, it has from its inception, been supplemented by a separate (Arabic) number system. However, it is more than coincidence that persons astute in "theomatics" have uncovered some profound computations when assigning numerical values in arithmetic progression of the value 6 to the English alphabet.

English, like the oldest alphabet discovered, is based on a root value of 6. For example, 6 x 2 = 1 foot; 6 x 6 = 1 yard; 6 "forties" = 1 section; 6 x 6 sections = 1 township. One township is a 6 mile square, etc.

"A" is derived from the ancient "Abba," meaning father, or man, whose number in the Scripture is 6. (See Age of Six). When the value of 6 is assigned to A, 12 to B, 18 to C, etc., many words relative to the Antichrist System equal 666. A few are (1), Mark of Beast = 666; (2), Computer = 666, (3), Kissinger, prototype of superb peace negotiator, = 666.

# The Great "Falling Away"

The "falling away first" (apostasia in Greek: defection from, revolt, religious apostacy) will evolve into a powerful One World Apostate Church. This is a necessary prerequisite for the "revealing" of the Antichrist.

These events must occur just prior to the beginning of the last seven years, as *he* (the "Other Christ") makes a covenant with the Jews for seven years that officially initiates Daniel's 70th week. Daniel 9:27.

# The World Won't Know Him!

A word of caution, this World Dictator will not be recognized as the Antichrist except by *informed* Christians! The world will be so intrigued by his words that it will be saying, "PEACE, PEACE"; "PEACE AND SAFETY."

The most *identifiable trait* of this coming "Man of Sin" will be his ability to negotiate a treaty of protection for Israel. *This treaty is already in its formative* stage. See chapter on "The Treaty." When the treaty is signed, the last seven years of this World Order will begin to tick off God's clock. Ladies and Gentlemen,

> *"How about your heart, is it right with God?*
> *That's the thing that counts today;*
> *Is it blacked by sin; it can be pure within,*
> *Won't you ask Christ in to stay?"*

"Peace and Safety," "War on the Saints,"
I Thessalonians 5:3; Daniel 7:21

## His Paradoxical Reign:
## Peace on Earth, War on Saints

Cronkite, Brinkley and Barbara Walters have been refused audiences with the "Other Christ." The world is euphoric. "Peace at last!" UPI picks up a news release in *The Jerusalem Post:*

> "Judaism has been endeavoring for centuries to convince the world that their Messiah, who has finally come, would be an ordinary man, anointed of God, and not one from heaven!"

> "The Lord thy God will raise up . . . a Prophet from the midst of thee, of thy brethren, like unto me, unto him ye shall hearken." Deuteronomy 18:15.

How sad for the world that the announcement stating that the "Other Christ" has come will be seven years premature! Sadder still for the Jews. Jesus Christ, the Prophet raised up in their midst, their real Messiah, had warned them afore time of this mistake:

> "I am come in my Father's name, and ye receive me not: *if another shall come in his own name,* him ye will receive." John 5:43.

Meanwhile, in heaven, the martyrs of the ages are crying, "Almighty Lord, holy and true! How long will it be until you judge the people of earth and punish them for killing us?" Revelation 6:10 TEB.

170

They are told to wait a little longer until their fellow servants of Christ and brethren would be killed as they were.

"The dragon (Satan) gave the beast his power and throne and great authority. I saw that one of his heads seemed wounded beyond recovery — but the fatal wound has healed! All the world marveled at this miracle and followed the Creature in awe. They worshiped the Dragon for giving him such power, and they worshiped the strange Creature. 'Where is there anyone as great as he?' they exclaimed. 'Who is able to fight against him?' Then the Dragon encouraged the Creature to speak great blasphemies against the Lord; and gave him authority to control the earth for forty-two months. All that time he blasphemed God's name and His temple and all those living in Heaven. The Dragon gave him power to fight against God's people and to overcome them, and to rule over all nations and language groups throughout the world. And all mankind — whose names were not written down before the founding of the world in the slain Lamb's Book of Life — worshiped the evil Creature. Anyone who can hear, listen carefully." Revelation 13:2-9 LB.

History does repeat itself! The Eighth World Government will presently give birth to another Babylon, the first real totalitarian government since Nebuchadnezzar . . . the head of gold, a King of

**Kings!** Daniel 2:37,38. At the outset of this seven-year regime, "power is given" the World Dictator over all "kindreds, tongues, and nations," Revelation 13:7; but three named things are specifically given into his hands: (1), Christians (2), times, and (3), laws; for a time, (1 year) times (2 years) and half a time (½ year); three and one-half years. We shall only discuss the first of these, Christians.

1. "He shall make war with the saints and prevail against them." Daniel 7:21.

2. "He shall wear out the saints of the most high." Daniel 7:25.

3. "The people that do know their God shall be strong, and do exploits. And they that understand among the people shall instruct many; yet they shall fall by the *sword* and by *flame*, by captivity, and spoil." Daniel 11:33.

4. "And it was given unto him to make war with the saints and to overcome them:" Revelation 13:7: But these things shall be "to try them, and to purge, and to make them white even to the time of the end." Daniel 11:35.

This absolute "power is given unto him to *continue* for 42 months," the first three and one-half year period.

While the world will be enjoying a measure of "Peace and Safety," Daniel 8:24 (buying, selling, planting, building, marrying, eating and drinking, Luke 17:26-30), the Christians will be driven "underground" by the new Caesar. History records the years of 117-180 A.D. as the most peaceful time the world has ever experienced. However, millions of Christians were being "eliminated," by the Roman Empire, all in the name of *peace!* This new Caesar, presented by the *Revived* Roman Empire again "by peace shall destroy many!" Daniel 8:25.

*This book is published by:*

Ministries, Inc.
Post Office Box 4038
Montgomery, Alabama 36104 (205) 262-4891

# CHAPTER IX

# MID WEEK

This World Dictator's utter wickedness will not be exposed to the world until the middle of this seven year period when the Ten European Nation Federation which hates the Apostate World Church (Revelation 17:16) that rode the Dictator to power (17:7) will destroy the One World Church.

With his headquarters at Mystery Babylon burned, the World Dictator: (1) Moves his capital to Jerusalem. Daniel 11:45, II Thessalonians 2:4. (2) Breaks his seven year treaty to protect Israel. Daniel 11:31, Daniel 9:27. (3) Sits in the Temple in Jerusalem and declares himself "God." II Thessalonians 2:4. (A) Forbids the Jews to sacrifice and render offerings to God. Daniel 9:27; 11:31; (B) Demands worship of the Jews, who had been the only people in the world the first three and one-half years not required to worship the "beast and his image"; but, under the treaty were allowed to continue to worship and sacrifice to their God. (Indeed, it is this provision of the treaty that induces them to sign it and convinces them that he is *their* Messiah.)

This World Dictator whose world power was absolute for the first three and one-half years:

1. For the first time is given a specific kingdom. (He has risen out of these Ten European Nations, but, he is another, an eleventh horn [king]. Daniel 7:8. These ten nations give their power to him, and he becomes their specific leader.) Revelation 17:17.

2. When he identifies with this Western Federation, his world prestige is lessened, and his power threatened. Daniel 11:40.

3. Will see *wars begin.* (The first three and one-half years the world experienced some degree of "peace and safety" [I Thessalonians 5:3] and Israel dwelt *safely.* Ezekiel 38:8, 11 & 14.)

(A) When he aligns himself with the West, the other powers in the world become incensed. *The South* pushes at him. Daniel 11:40. Note here, how specific the time element is. Daniel 11:40, "at the time *'of the end,'* " the King of the South . . . "Of the end" in Hebrew means "extreme end." The extreme end (the last three and one-half years) begins with wars. *Christians notice* in Daniel 11:32-35, the Church will endure severe persecutions (Tribulation) "to try them, and to purge, and to make them white, even *to* the time *'of the end,'* " same exact term in Hebrew. Tribulation will last only the first three and one-half years *to* the time of the end when the wrath of God begins.

(B) In addition to the *King of the South* pushing; the *King of the North* will come against him with chariots and horsemen, and many ships. This battle synchronizes with Gog and Magog and her allies of Ezekiel 38. (If Russia had marched on Israel to begin this seven year period they could not have recovered in three and one-half years losing five/sixth of their army sufficiently to come against anyone.

(C) As the Northern Federation and her allies come against Israel here in midweek, the Jews will experience these last three and one-half years what the Christians did the first three and one-half years; "purging." The first period will see the Antichrist trying to exterminate the Church; (But it will only purify it . . . when Christ returns to take the Church out, it will be without "spot or wrinkle or any such thing)." The last three and one-half years will see Antichrist making the last attempt at exterminating the Jews.

(D) Also war "tidings out of the *East* shall trouble him."

4. The abomination of desolation* will occur in midweek, and the Jews will flee to the place providentially provided for them. (I have seen pictures of cave houses dug back into moun-

---

* Abomination of desolation is the desecration of the Temple in Jerusalem, about which both Daniel and Jesus spoke. Daniel 9:27; 11:28; and Matthew 24:15. It occurs in the middle of the seven year period at which time the Antichrist will exalt himself above all Gods (II Thessalonians 2:3-8); and demand a cessation of Jewish sacrifices and offerings, and their worship of himself. This will bring about the final desolation of Israel according to Ezekiel, chapters 7-10.

176

tainous regions being stocked with food and supplies for this very time.) It appears only one-half of one-third of the Jews living in Israel at this time shall escape death.

"And it shall come to pass in *all* the land, . . . two parts *therein* shall die *in* Israel, but the third shall be left therein. And I will bring the third part *through the fire,* and will refine them as silver is refined, and will try them as gold is tried: . . . I will gather all nations against Jerusalem to battle, . . . and half of the city shall go into captivity, *and the residue of the people shall not be* cut off from the city." Zechariah 13:8; 14:2.

(What tribulation does for the Christians the first three and one-half years is to get them ready to be "caught up to meet the Lord in the air," Jacob's trouble will do for the few Jews left readying them to meet their real Messiah "with all his saints," when his feet shall stand in that day upon the Mount of Olives. Zechariah 14:4-5. These few purified Jews will go into the Millennium in their physical bodies to propagate the land of Israel under King David. Ezekiel 37:24.)

There are so many dear people who have such a vague concept of the "abomination of desolation," that I feel impressed to share with you what takes place in the Temple, and Jerusalem at this time. Excerpts from the Living Bible except as noted, from chapter 7:3 to 9:7.

"Now is the end come upon thee, and I will send mine anger upon thee, and will judge thee according to thy ways and will recompense upon thee all thine abominations. And mine eye shall not spare thee, neither will I have pity. . . . Now will I shortly pour out my fury upon thee, and accomplish mine anger upon thee: and I will judge thee according to thy ways, and will recompense thee for all thine abominations . . . and ye shall know that I am the Lord that smiteth . . . *for wrath is upon all the multitude* . . . But, they that escape . . . shall be on the mountains like doves . . . all of them mourning, everyone for his iniquity. They shall cast their silver in the streets, and their gold shall be removed: *their silver and their gold shall not be able to deliver them in the day of the wrath of the Lord.*"

(These last three and one-half years will be the *WRATH OF GOD!* Buying and selling will continue to the Lord's coming for the Church, Luke 17:26-30; at midweek; after which silver and gold will become worthless. Zephaniah 1:18 confirms Ezekiel 7:19; "Neither their silver nor their gold shall be able to deliver them in the day of the Lord's wrath.")

"My face *will I turn also from them, and they shall pollute my secret* place: for the *robbers shall enter into it, and defile it. Destruction cometh;* and they shall seek peace, and there shall be none." KJV.

"He said to me, 'Son of dust, look toward the north,' So I looked and, sure enough, north of the altar gate, in the entrance, stood the idol. And he said: 'Son of dust, do you see what they are doing? Do you see what great sins the people of Israel are doing here, *to push me from my Temple?* But come, and I will show you greater sins than these!' Then he brought me to the door of the Temple court, where I made out an opening in the wall, so I went in. The walls were covered with pictures of all kinds of snakes, lizards and hideous creatures, besides all the various idols worshiped by the people of Israel. He brought me to the north gate of the Temple, and there sat women weeping for Tammuz, their god. 'Have you seen this?' he asked. 'But I will show you greater evils than these!' Then he brought me into the inner court of the Temple and there at the door, between the porch and the bronze altar, were about 25 men standing with their backs to the Temple of the Lord, facing east, worshiping the sun! And the glory of the God of Israel rose from the cherubim where it had rested and stood above the entrance to the Temple. And the Lord called to the man with the writer's case, and said to him, 'Walk through the streets of Jerusalem and put a mark on the foreheads of the men who weep and sigh because of all the sins they see around them.' Then I heard the Lord tell the other men: 'Follow him through the city and kill everyone whose forehead isn't marked. Spare not nor pity them. Kill them all, old and young, girls, women and little children; but don't touch anyone with the *mark. And begin right here at the Temple.'* And so they began by killing the seventy elders. And he said, *'Defile the Temple!* Fill its courts with the bodies of those you kill! Go! And they went out through the city and did as they were told!' "

(This marking corresponds to the sealing of the 144,000 in Revelation, chapter 7, which happens when the church is taken out; wars and the wrath of God commence in mid-week simultaneously.)

5. The reign of Antichrist will continue through the last three and one-half years, and although his power is diluted, he will still enjoy success even to the end of the period. "And the king shall do according to his will; . . . and *shall prosper* until the indignation be accomplished." "The king will do what he chooses; . . . *All will go well* for him until the time of *wrath ends."* Daniel 11:36 KJV & NEB (see more on this period of wrath in last chapter).

*This book is published by:*

Ministries, Inc.
Post Office Box 4038
Montgomery, Alabama 36104 (205) 262-4891

# CHAPTER X

# THE LAST SEVEN YEARS

## Epilogue

Soon after the death of my husband, I began to experience being "married to Christ" in another dimension. I was spending ten to sixteen hours a day in the word concurrently with studying systematic theological thought relative to the subjects I was pursuing. I would go to bed with the scriptures, sometimes several versions lying open on "my husband's side." My Heavenly Bridegroom began breathing new life through these pages. For more than 25 years I had been a serious student of the Bible, memorizing significant portions of the Old Testament and much more of the New Testament. I literally "wore out" to the point of falling apart four different Bibles. Many mornings I would rise early as 2:30 A.M., and start memorizing the Word. To the married, I say, "You cannot understand this dimension. You go to bed and arise (and rightfully!) communicating and interacting with your spouse." I experienced a shift of these energies into an even *greater* drive "to *know Him.*" Many times in fervent prayer and consultation with the Lord, I would find myself assessing a measure of success, education, business, and wealth; then saying with Paul, "What things were gain to me, those I count loss for Christ." Yes, "I count all things but loss for the excellency of the *knowledge of Christ Jesus my Lord:* for whom I have suffered the loss of all things, and do count them but dung, that I may . . . *know him,* and the *power of his resurrection, and the fellowship of his sufferings"* (sufferings that have seen the Lord of my life remove every member of my immediate family: my husband, my precious live-in housekeeper of many years, and my only child, a twenty-seven-year-old son, all within these past two and one-half years). Most of us desire *to know Him* only in the "power of His resurrection, but not in the fellowship of His sufferings." The unpopular truth is that "we are not only to believe on Him, but also to suffer for His sake." During these months, there began to surface a relentless drive to take the prophecies, which make up about one-third of the Bible, and sequence them chronologically; preceding, during, and following Daniel's 70th week, or the last seven years of this World Order.

I set myself to seek the Lord until the task was completed. I made no business or social engagements, not even on Thanksgiving Day. I literally lived like a monk for three and one-half months, seven days a week, twelve to sixteen hours a day.

This particular study became the first of three, which I conducted in the past two years, each continuing for a little more than three months.

The study was motivated by one insatiable desire — to know the truth concerning the time of the end. I had no bones to pick with anyone. I had no denominational alignment that I was seeking to augment. Publicity is something I avidly avoid. Publishing a book was the remotest thing from my mind. Significantly, my income did not need to be supplemented.

Years ago in my reading, a few things became obvious to me:

1. *Fear* the writer whose research is oriented toward selling books; catchy titles — no substance.

2. *Question* the writer who depends upon the sale of books as a primary source of his income.

3. *Reject* the person whose writings extol only the goodness of God . . . the best selling subjects. Paul warned the Ephesians and the Romans in Acts 20:25-27, and Romans 11:22, that when the time came that ''ye shall see my face no more I shall be pure of the blood of all men having not shunned to declare unto you *all* the counsel of God; having taught you to behold both the *goodness* and the *severity* of God.'' Then he quickly added, ''Some of you yourselves will distort the truth in order to draw a following.'' Acts 20:30 LB.

4. Love and understand the person who writes for or ministers in a particular denomination

183

from which he is being financially supported. He is unconsciously prejudiced! To be open to the truth which might put him at variance with the doctrine he has agreed to uphold will put him in a quandary. He will either become miserable supporting a doctrine he does not believe; or he will become financially deprived having to detach himself from the denomination. So ignorance remains bliss and "truth is fallen in the street." Isaiah 59:14.

5. God will reveal pure truths only to a person who can disassociate his pursuit from the "money motive."

6. A little truth sprinkled with error is more dangerous than untruth, for it is more believable.

7. The Bible contains many paradoxes, not the least of which is: "The truth shall set you free," but "knowledge increases sorrow."

8. Before you can establish a balanced view of a scriptural truth, you must lift out and examine *every parallel passage* in the Bible. "A text without a context is a pretext." You can not then interpret any one passage in a way that is repugnant to *any* of the many other passages, or you are guilty of violating the most basic principle of Bible Hermeneutics, the Principle of Harmony. It has been my privilege to teach Bible Hermeneutics, both General and Special; and the most basic

184

concept one must learn to apply is that *no one scripture stands* as an island to itself; but, must be fit into the "seven continents before its contribution to the whole can be assessed!"

9. The many prophecies may seem like a symposium with many and varied contributors; but, all of them emanate from one author; the Holy Spirit, who made certain those persons through whom He spoke would just "report" and not "edit."

10. The true prophetic messages rarely ever evoked a pleasant response, and were invariably delivered at the peril of the prophet's reputation, and at times his life. A balanced teaching of these prophetic messages today will reveal that the pattern of response has not been substantially altered.

And now, Brothers and Sisters in Christ, some of the things I have written in prior chapters, I honestly confessed were "prudent assessments." I must now make a radical departure and commend to you that which is contained in this chapter relevant to the Overall Structuring of Daniel's 70th Week is Divine Revelation! The same Holy Ghost who moved Holy men of old to "write the things that shall be hereafter" moved on me divinely revealing to me what it was He originally spoke to them!

And now, I submit unto the Father of our Lord Jesus Christ a fervent prayer for *Divine Illumination* of the Holy Ghost on your behalf, enabling you to interpret those things given to me by *Divine Revelation* by the Holy Ghost, of the things originally spoken through the prophets by *Divine Inspiration* of the Holy Ghost. Amen! Amen!

I now "humble myself under the mighty hand of God, and submit myself to the Lord," even as I do daily, and submit myself to each of you in the body of Christ, cognizant that I come to you in the role of a servant of all. Yet, unashamedly acknowledging that for many years, I have diligently and studiously sought Heaven's most coveted disposition, "to prophesy" (I Corinthians 14:39), that I might speak God's "untainted" truths. "Finally brethren," I am aware that the hour has come; and that God has indeed "brought me to the Kingdom for just such a time as this" and to this very Chapter in which I boldly confess that I come to you in the role of a New Testament "Prophet." ". . . In the last days . . . your sons and your daughters shall prophesy." Acts 2:17. Prophesy = propheteia in Greek, which literally means "to declare forth the mind and counsel of God."

### Great Tribulation Versus the Wrath of God

I have sought to be divinely endued with the ability to condense what should be a three-hundred-page treatise to the barest basics and yet retain continuity.

Most Christians have been taught that there would be a seven-year period divided in the middle that would end this World Order. *This is truth.* Likewise, most Christians have been taught that this entire seven-year period is "The Great Tribulation." This is untruth,

186

and one of the greatest misnomers ever perpetrated upon Bible believing Christians. Here we have a tremendous truth, followed by a false premise, the combination of which has yielded mass confusion in Christianity. Daniel's 70th week consists of two distinct periods of 1260 days (plus 75 days). War against the saints (The Great Tribulation) only lasts 42 months, (1260 days). Daniel 7:21 & 25; Revelation 13:5. The latter period is the Wrath of God, (Jacob's Trouble). There is NOT ONE SCRIPTURE that refers to a ''SEVEN-YEAR TRIBULATION PERIOD.''

It was in my third week of categorizing the prophetic scriptures into their sequential order of this seven-year period, praying concurrently night and day that the Holy Ghost would ''teach me all things,'' that He spoke with a clarion sound inwardly, interrupting my sequence, ''As it was in the days of Noe . . . as it was in the days of Lot . . .'' I looked up Luke 17:26-29:

> ''And as it was in the days of Noe, so shall it be also in the days of the Son of man. They did eat, they drank, they married wives, they were given in marriage, until the *day* that *Noe* entered into the *ark* and the flood came, and *destroyed them all.* Likewise also as it was in the days of Lot; they did eat, they drank, they bought, they sold, they planted, they builded; But the *same day* that *Lot* went out of Sodom it rained *fire* and *brimstone from Heaven* and *destroyed them all.*''

187

I went back to Genesis, chapters six and nineteen. I then researched every scriptural reference about the days of Noah and Lot. After many hours I concluded:

1. There would be *food and drink available to the very day of Christ's return!* In other words, no worldwide famine will herald His return; only "famines in different places." Matthew 24:7.

2. There would be people falling in love and marrying to the very day of His coming. There would be no generalized thought in their minds of an imminent end to the age. Marriage denotes long-term planning; establishing homes, having children . . . counting on tomorrow as today.

3. There would be subcultures (Sodom) that would eat and drink, but notably missing from their culture would be marriage, presupposing sexually perverted societies.

4. There would be *"buying* and *selling"*; indicating there would be *goods and means with which to buy them to the very day of His return.* Contrast this to Ezekiel 7:19.

5. There would be planting to the day of His return; planting with the thought of harvesting in a few months.

6. There would be building; building expecting to live in the houses for years. There would be absolutely no thoughts of a sudden "end of this age" in the mind of the world; but, as

Noah and Lot knew all about it, so will the Church.

7.　To the people of the world, Christ will come as a "thief in the night." Noah, a believer knew about the end of his age, but could not convince the world. The flood came as a shock to the old world, though they were exposed to the truth! As Lot, a believer was apprised of the end, so will the Christians be apprised. And as Lot could not persuade even his sons-in-law who mocked him in disbelief, Christians will be unable to convince even members of their own families who will mock in disbelief even to the very day of Christ's return.

He will therefore come as a thief in the night to the world (although often exposed to the truth), but not as a thief in the night to the believers. I Thessalonians 5:1-4, "But of the times and the seasons, brethren, ye have no need that I write unto you. For yourselves know perfectly that the day of the Lord so cometh *as a thief* in the night. For when *they* (the world) shall say, Peace and safety; then sudden destruction cometh upon *them* (the world), as travail upon a woman with child; and they (the world) shall not escape. *But ye, brethren,* are not in darkness, that that day should overtake you as a thief." Note: the thief in the night in verse two is "they"; the believer in verse four is "you brethren."

8.  ". . . until the *day* that *Noe* entered into the *ark*, and the *flood* came, and *destroyed them all*."  This was the first great breakthrough in the study! I had never seen this before, although a long time before I had memorized the Scripture! The *day* representing Christ's coming for the church, *Noah* (representing the believer) entered into the *ark* (representing the place prepared for us) the *flood* (representing the wrath of God) came and destroyed them all (representing a doomed world). *Not one person other than Noah and his family was saved.* The remainder of the world immediately received the Wrath of God from which there was no escape.

9.  The same *day* that *Lot* went out of *Sodom* it rained *fire and brimstone from Heaven and destroyed them all.* The day (analogizing the day of Christ's coming) *Lot* (analogizing the believer) went out of *Sodom* (the corrupt world) it rained fire and brimstone (analogizing the Wrath of God from Heaven) and destroyed them all (analogizing the doomed world)! No exceptions! No more repentance. No one "giving their life for their testimony!"

*CHURCH, BEWARE!* Jesus Christ gave only two precedents as analogies of His coming for *His Church.* Noah and Lot.

*CHRISTIANS, BEWARE!* Stop substituting your words "as it was in the days of Enoch and Elijah!" for

190

the words of Jesus Christ! The penalty for "adding unto" or "taking away from" the truths of God is severe! Revelation 22:18,19.

When this great concept was revealed to me; that whenever Christ comes for His Bride, there would be no one else saved, I was *so shaken* by the false teachings of the millions saved after the "catching away"; the multitudes the 144,000 sealed Jews would win, that I literally detached myself from every teaching, doctrine, or belief I had embraced and as a raft floats in the ocean, I became free to be blown about by the wind of Heaven, the Holy Spirit of God!

Even as I prayed many, many times, I pause and pray again at this moment, "O Holy Spirit, Spirit of Truth, thou Breath of God, thou Wind of Heaven, come and blow upon your servant until all the chaff of untruthfulness is carried away, and continue to blow until only the full grown kernel of truth remains; for the 'fan is in your hand, and you will thoroughly purge your floor; and the *wheat* you will gather into your garner, but, the chaff you will burn with fire un-quenchable!' "

At this juncture in my study, I did not know if the "catching away" would be prior to, at, during, or after the close of this seven-year period. I knew that "the Holy Ghost would show me," if I continued to persevere, for "He is a rewarder of those who deli-gently seek him."

## The Wrath of God

The next great concept revealed to me was that the *Wrath of God* was never sent on believers. God

191

chastens, permits afflictions, persecutions, and tribulation to "try, purge, and make white, even as silver is refined in the furnace;" but, we are instructed to "wait for His Son from Heaven . . . even Jesus, which hath *delivered* us from *the wrath to come.*" I Thessalonians 1:10. The term "delivered" in Greek is rhuomai, meaning "to rescue." His coming is therefore "to rescue" us from the wrath to come; NIV uses this rendering. "God hath not appointed us to wrath, but to obtain salvation . . . Wherefore *comfort* yourselves together." I Thessalonians 5:9&11. Why? For we have received salvation from the "Wrath of God!"

After many hours of referencing this term, "Wrath of God," I was able to firmly establish these premises which I shall reduce to a bare minimum here.

1. That this was a distinct period of time yet in the future alluded to more than a hundred times by many different terms in Hebrew and Greek, translated many different ways, including the "Day of the Lord."

2. That it was to begin in Revelation 6:17; "For the great day of His wrath is come, and who shall be able to stand?"

3. That it is to follow the great tribulation of the saints which has a duration of "time (one year), times (two years), and the dividing of time (one-half year)"; three and one-half years. ( (X) (2X) (X) = 42 months).

2

"I beheld, and the same horn made war with the

saints, and prevailed against them; And he shall speak great words against the most High, and shall *wear* out the saints of the most High, and think to change times and laws: and they shall be given into his hand until *a time and times and the dividing of time.*" Daniel 7:21&25.

"And there was given unto him a mouth speaking great things and blasphemies; and power was given unto him *to continue forty and two months.* And he opened his mouth in blasphemy against God, to blaspheme his name, and his tabernacle, and them that dwell in Heaven. And it was given unto him to make war with the saints, and to overcome them: and power was given him over all kindreds and tongues, and nations." Revelation 13:5-7. The key word in Revelation 13:5, is to "continue" which means to "make war," which is against the saints, and this lasts forty-two months.

Therefore, by process of simple deduction, the Wrath of God transpires during the last three and one-half years of Daniel's 70th week, or the last three and one-half years of this World Order.

## Tribulation

I now turned my undivided attention to a study of Tribulation. "Thilipsis" in Greek literally means, and can be translated, pressure, affliction, and persecution. I was surprised to learn that the Church had been in it in varying degrees since the healing of the lame man by the gate Beautiful, in Acts, chapter three. Let us look at a few references:

"In the world ye shall have *tribulation.*" John 16:33.

"We must through much *tribulation* enter into the Kingdom of God." Acts 14:22.

"We glory in *tribulation.*" Romans 5:3.

"Shall *tribulation* or distress, or persecution, or famine, or nakedness, or peril, or sword . . . separate us from the love of Christ?" Romans 8:35.

"Who comforteth us in all our *tribulation* that we may be able to comfort them which are in any trouble . . . For as the *sufferings* of Christ abound in us, so our consolation also aboundeth by Christ. For we would not, brethren have you ignorant of our *trouble* which came to us in Asia, that we were *pressed out of measure,* above strength, insomuch that we despaired even of life: But, we had the sentence *of death in ourselves,* that we should not trust in ourselves, but in God which raiseth the dead: Who delivered us from so great a death, and doth deliver: in whom we trust that he will yet deliver us." II Corinthians 1:4,5,8,9,10.

"I am exceeding joyful in all our *tribulation.* For when we were come into Macedonia, our flesh had no rest, but we were troubled on every side; without were fightings within were fears." II Corinthians 7:4-5.

"I desire that ye faint not at my *tribulation* for you." Ephesians 3:13.

"That no man should be moved by *these afflictions:* for yourselves know that we are appointed thereunto. For verily, when we were with you, we told you before that we should suffer *tribulation;* even as it came to pass, and ye know. For this cause, when I could no longer forbear, I sent to know your faith, lest by some means the tempter have tempted you, and our labour be in vain." I Thessalonians 3:3-5. Note here, tribulations are sent by Satan!

"So that we ourselves glory in you in the churches of God for your patience and faith in all your persecutions and tribulations that ye endure: which is a *manifest token of the righteous judgment of God, that ye may be counted worthy of the Kingdom of God, for which ye also suffer:"* II Thessalonians 1:4,5.

"I John, who also am your brother, and companion in *tribulation,* and in the kingdom and patience of Jesus Christ, was in the isle that is called Patmos, for the word of God, and for the testimony of Jesus Christ." Revelation 1:9.

". . . these are they which came out of great tribulation." Revelation 7:14.

After Revelation 7:14, when the saints are in heaven, the term does not appear again in scripture; but the Wrath of God takes over appearing thirteen times from Revelation 6:16 to Revelation 19:15, during which time "they repented not" is repeated three times.

I researched the systematic theological thoughts on the subject of tribulation from the time of the Early Church Fathers.

Irenaeus (ca. 140-202) Bishop of Lyons, disciple of Polycarp, tutored by the Apostle John is reflective of early Christian thought about the last "great tribulation:"

> "And therefore, when in the end the Church shall be suddenly caught up from this earth, it is said, 'There shall be tribulation such as has not been since the beginning neither shall be,'
> For this is the last contest of the *righteous* in which, when they overcome, they are crowned with incorruption." *Irenaeus, Against Heresies Book V,* chapter xxix, page 558.

Irenaeus further synchronized the "catching away" with the *first resurrection* of Revelation 20:4-6, as he taught that the resurrection of the just will take place *after* the coming of the Antichrist. Ibid.

To condense historical theology into a capsule is to arrive at one conclusion: The fundamental Church Fathers down through the ages were Pre-Millennial in their teaching of the Rapture. They were Post-Tribulation, and deductively Pre-Wrath.

Some weeks after the Holy Spirit revealed to me the correct structuring of Daniel's 70th week; that is, the first three and one-half years as the Great Tribulation, and the last three and one-half years as the Wrath of God; the Lord's "catching out" the Church after the Tribulation, but prior to the Wrath of God, I felt like an unwanted misfit. The truth had been revealed to me, but the real truth was, no one would want to hear it. I came to my study and wept all morning. I said to God, "Oh! that I could unlearn what I know. No one wants to know what I know for I wish that I didn't know it myself." The Lord reminded me of the dozens of times I wept before Him, pleading with Him to "open up the secrets of the end time to me." I finally cried to the Lord, "All right, I know now; but don't, please don't ever require me to teach it!"

I pondered here in my study on whom else the Holy Spirit had revealed this truth. "Let every word (issue) be established by two or three witnesses." I have learned when the wind of the Holy Ghost begins to blow in one direction, much of the wheat begins bending downwind. When I got up from the floor where I had been weeping, praying, and talking with the Lord about this, I walked as though drawn by a magnet to a wall of my study lined with books, pulled out one I had never opened, placed there by a minister friend entitled *Explore The Book*. It is written by a renowned contemporary theologian, Dr. J. Sidlow Baxter. I immediately turned to read his treatment of the Revelation, and found myself staring in almost disbelief at page 345 which he captions, *"Great Tribulation"* versus *"Wrath of God."*

"In this parallel there is one feature which is peculiarly arresting when once it is perceived, namely, the solemn pause between the seven

197

seals and the seven trumpets in column one, and the correspondingly solemn break between the seven personages and the seven vials in column two. (See in the one case vi. 17-viii. I, and in the other case xiii. 18-xv. I.) Why, then, this break between seals and trumpets, and before the vials? *It is to mark a distinction between the two stages of the age-end crisis, i.e. between the oft-called 'Great Tribulation' and the 'Wrath of God.' We cannot recall having seen this distinction pointed out before in expositions of New Testament eschatology,* yet it is certainly there (not only in the Apocalypse, but in other Scriptures too: see Matthew xxiv. 29-31), and has an illuminating bearing upon the question as to whether the Church will or will not go through the 'Great Tribulation.' Again and again we meet persons who hold the common idea that the church will have been transplanted to Heaven before the 'Great Tribulation' develops on earth, yet to us their main reason for so believing seems doubtful. They say: 'We cannot think that the Church could possibly be left on earth during those awful few years which end the present age, because that will be the time when the judgments and wrath of God are poured down upon the earth; and how could the Church be allowed on earth to undergo all that, since the cross of Christ has saved believers from such judgment?'

''Yet there are passages in the New Testament which to our own mind certainly seem to show *that believers of the last days* (there is only one small part of the total Church on earth at any given moment) will be on earth during the so-called 'Great Tribulation.' II Thessalonians ii is one such . . . *we do suggest that there is one fact which has hitherto been overlooked, namely, that the 'Great Tribulation' and the 'Wrath of God' are not identical.* When Christians say they cannot think that the Church could be left on earth during the 'Great Tribulation' because it is then that the 'wrath to come' is poured out, *they are confusing things which differ. That 'Wrath of God' is the last, awful end-bit which 'immediately follows'* (Matthew xxiv. 29) the 'Great Tribulation.' Now certainly no blood-bought, Spirit-sealed member of our Lord's mystic body can be thought of as left on earth and undergoing that. Yet it is quite possible — and from some passages in the New Testament seems (to us) necessarily implied — that believers will still be here during the 'Great Tribulation' when the 'man of sin' is here . . . Remember, the *'Great Tribulation' is largely of Satanic instigation through the 'man of sin,'* whereas the *'Wrath of God'* is entirely an affliction from God Himself. When the 'Great Tribulation' and the 'Wrath of God' are treated as identical, confusion results.''

In addition, Mr. John T. Sharrit, President of Christian Missionary Society, published a book in

1978 entitled, *Soon Coming World Shaking Events.*
Mr. Sharrit indicates in this publication that the Holy
Spirit revealed to him these same basic truths.

## The Resurrection

Now, in an attempt to clarify a few other classic er-
rors being propagated, let me summarize some of my
findings:

The Pre-Tribulation Theory has *no resurrection!*
The first resurrection of Revelation 20:4-6 is the only
resurrection of the just, for the only coming of Christ
for the Church. (His coming back to the earth is *with
all* the saints.) Zechariah 14:5. Many have manufactured abberrations of the scriptures teaching firstfruits,
gleanings, and harvesting resurrections. Hear therefore, what the scriptures say:

"Marvel not at this for the hour is coming, in
the which all that are in the graves shall hear
his voice. And shall come forth; they that
have done good, unto *the resurrection of life;*
and they that have done evil, unto the resurrection of damnation." John 5:28-29.

"For thou shalt be recompensed at *the resurrection of the just.*" Luke 14:14.

". . . And have hope toward God, which they
themselves also allow, that there shall be *a*
resurrection of the dead, both of the *just* and
*unjust.*"

Jesus here taught about (1) *The resurrection* of
life and the *resurrection* of damnation. (2) The *Resur-*

*rection of the just.* (3) Paul here taught ''there would'' be *a resurrection* of the just, and *a resurrection* of the unjust. The indefinite articles ''the and a'' are correctly translated out of the Greek and always denote singularity — one of its kind!

When the Principle of Harmony is applied to every parallel passage about the resurrection, all must agree. When one takes an unabridged concordance and checks out every reference, one will discover that there is *a resurrection* of the just, and *a resurrection of the unjust.*

''And I saw thrones, and they sat upon them, and judgment was given unto them: and I saw the souls of them, that were beheaded for the witness of Jesus, and for the word of God, *and which had not worshiped the beast, neither his image, neither had received his mark upon their foreheads, or in their hands; and they lived and reigned with Christ a thousand years.* But the rest of the dead lived not again until the thousand years were finished. This is *the first* resurrection. Blessed and holy is he that hath part in the first resurrection: on such the second death hath no power, but they shall be priests of God and of Christ, and shall reign with him a thousand years.'' Revelation 20:4-6. *NOTE:* The saints whom the Antichrist warred against and overcame, are in this *first resurrection!* The only resurrection left is one thousand years later.

Let us look at the resurrection in I Corinthians 15:51-52,

"Behold, I shew you a mystery; We shall not all sleep, but we shall all be changed. In a moment, in the twinkling of an eye, at the *last* trump: for the trumpet shall sound, and the dead shall be raised incorruptible, and we shall be changed."

When does this occur? "At the *last* trump." Since it says the *"last trump"* there could not be a later one. Since there is only *one resurrection* for the just, it is here at the "last trump." Some say that this "catching away" is at the beginning of this seven-year period. They have, therefore, used the *"last* trump"; and the "only resurrection" for the just. How can they invent another trump later than the last one? How are they going to get the Great Tribulation saints raised? The Scriptures teach that these *are in the first Resurrection!* I am trying not to be facetious, but I admit that this multiple resurrection theory is so fabricated that in one of my books on the Pre-Trib Doctrine, the author suggests that this "last trump will toot twice!" I have not found those "two toots" in the Bible yet!

Let us continue to look at the resurrection. "For the Lord himself shall descend from heaven with a *shout,* with a voice of the *archangel,* and with the *trump* of God: and the dead in Christ shall rise first: Then we which are alive and remain shall be caught up together with them in the *clouds* to meet the Lord in the air: and so shall we ever be with the Lord. Wherefore comfort one another with these words." I Thessalonians 4:16-18. *This coming* for the Church is going to be accompanied by a *shout, voice* of the archangel, and the *trump* of God . . . ("the last trump"). In the margins of almost every reference Bible (Thompson's New Chain Reference, Holman Regal Reference, even the small Cambridge University Press) is written out beside Matthew 24:31, a reference to I Corinthians 15:52; I Thessalonians 4:16, Last Trump, indicating these three Scriptures speak of the same event, the coming of Christ for the Church. "And he shall send his angels with a great *sound* of a *trumpet,* and they shall gather together his *elect* from the four winds, from one end of heaven to the other. The *trumpet and sound are one and the same with the trumpet and sound of I Corinthians 15:51* and I Thessalonians 4:16; and *further amplification is made in Thompson's that the trump of Matthew 24:31, means 'last trump' of I Thessalonians 4:16!* Actually the Greek term Salpinx from which all these references are translated includes: trump, shout and great voice." This is indeed the Feast of Trumpets. Thus the "catching away" of the Church is properly sequenced as our Lord taught it in Matthew 24:29.

"Immediately after the tribulation of those days . . . then shall appear the sign of the Son of man in Heaven . . . and He shall send His angels with a great sound . . ." The "catching away" after the tribulation of those days synchronizes with the "first resurrection" of Revelation 20:4-6!

# The 24 "Elders"

In a further effort to substantiate the modern Pre-Trib Rapture Theory, these advocates must get the Church into Heaven prior to Revelation 7:9, when the Tribulation Saints are seen. They therefore teach that the "Church" is caught away in Revelation 4:1, and is seen in Heaven in the form of the twenty-four elders in Revelation 5:9. *Neither can be true!* This teaching can not go beyond the King James Version without falling into total disrepute, as it is predicated on an error in the translation! Look at the twenty-four elders (the supposed Church) in the King James Version.

> "And they sung a new song, saying, Thou art worthy to take the book, and to open the seals thereof: for thou wast slain, and hast redeemed *us* to God by thy blood out of every kindred, and tongue, and people, and nation; And hast made *us* unto our God Kings and Priests: and *we* shall reign on the earth." Revelation 5:9.

The entire Pre-Trib Teaching is predicated on these pronouns, redeemed "*us*," made "*us*," "*we* shall reign." Every pronoun is a King James Version translation error!

*All subsequent versions,* which are too numerous to name, corrected this error made by the King James Version, and correctly translates the pronouns into either second or third person. Typical is the Revised Standard Version, which says: "ransom men," "gathered them," and "they" (not "we") shall reign.

"And they sang a new song, saying, 'Worthy art Thou to take the book, and to break its seals; for Thou was slain, and didst purchase for God with Thy blood *men from every tribe and tongue* and *people* and *nation.* And Thou has made *them* to be a kingdom and priests to our God; and *they* will reign upon the earth.' " NAS.

May God help us when our beliefs are so spurious that they are totally devastated by corrected translations. The sequence of His coming for the Church in Revelation is:

"And when he had opened the fifth seal, I saw under the altar the souls of them that were slain for the word of God, and for the testimony which they held: And they cried with a loud voice, saying, How long, O Lord, holy and true, dost thou not judge and avenge our blood on them that dwell on the earth? And white robes were given unto every one of them; and it was said unto them, that they should rest yet for a little season, until their fellow-servants also and their brethren, that should be killed as they were, should be fulfilled." Revelation 6:9-11.

The multitudes who had been martyrs throughout the ages right up to the time of the Great Tribulation, but specifically excluding those yet to be martyred by the Antichrist; compare Revelation 6:9, with Revelation 20:4, where the first part of 20:4 includes the class of martyrs of 6:9; then the conjunction *and;* which then distinguishes the Antichrist's martyrs in addition. This 6:9 multitude is told to wait a little season or for the three and one-half years Great Tribulation martyrs to be killed; then Christ would come for the Church.

Christ comes after the opening of the Sixth Seal in Revelation 6:12; which corresponds to His coming in Matthew 24:30; Mark 13:24, Luke 21:27, I Thessalonians 4:16, I Corinthians 15:51, etc., all hermeneutically harmonious.

Immediately, after His coming in Revelation 6:16, people began to pray to the mountains to hide them from the Wrath of the Lamb; ''for the great day of His Wrath is come, and who shall be able to stand?'' The tribulation has ended; the Church is ''caught up''; but, the Wrath of God, (the flood of Noah's day from which no one escaped) is come, and will destroy the doomed world.

If any of you have ever contemplated being saved after the Church is taken out, don't depend on it. ''Today is the day of Salvation.''

Seeing that there will be no one else saved, God provides another method of preserving the 144,000 Jews. He seals them in Revelation, chapter seven. They are seen again on Mt. Sion with Christ in Revelation 14:1; but their *number has remained fixed!* There is no Scripture to indicate that they become ''flaming evangels,'' and win millions during this period. A few

Jews (one-half of one-third) will go into the Millennium in their physical bodies. Zechariah 13:8 to 14:3; Ezekiel 37.

The two witnesses these last three and one-half years have no converts. Only ''they repented not'' three times occurs after the Church is taken out.

The Church is seen in Heaven the first time in Revelation 7:14-17. Christ comes back ''*with all* His saints'' three and one-half years later (after the Wrath of God is finished, as seen in Revelation 19, Jude 14, and Zechariah 14:5). No saints have been on earth during this time! There are no saints here to greet Him! He brings ''all the saints'' back with Him.

## The Church of Philadelphia

Will the Church of Philadelphia be kept *from* the hour of temptation?

''Because thou has kept the word of my patience, I also will keep thee *from* the hour of temptation, which shall come upon all the world, to try them that dwell upon the earth.'' Revelation 3:10.

Four times during this initial three and one-half month period, the Lord gave me ''supernatural'' revelations, ''in visions or dreams'' by night as I was asleep. The first one came about four weeks into the study and for brevity's sake, I shall just say that it was communicated to me that all seven churches have concurrently constituted the whole of Christianity down through the ages and are present in Contemporary

Christendom today.

I had looked into the Ephesus to Laodicean epoch theory. I failed to find one Scriptural allusion to it. However, if one could know positively that the Philadelphia Church is the Church of today that will be "caught away," let us examine the words "keep thee *from* the hour."

Moffat says:

"It is impossible from the grammar and difficult from the sense to decide whether terein en means successful endurance (pregnant sense as in John 17:15) or absolute immunity (cf. II Peter 2:9), safe emergence from the trial or escape from it entirely."

Kenneth Taylor says in Living Prophecies,

"The inference is not clear in the Greek, as to whether this means 'kept from' or 'kept through' " (the tribulation).

### The Escape From All These Things

These are our Lord's words in Luke 21:36,

"Watch ye therefore, and pray always, that ye may be accounted worthy to *escape* all these things that *shall* come to pass, and to *stand* before the Son of man."

Note: "Escape" in the *Expository Dictionary of New Testament Words* is "Ekpheugo; to flee *out of* a place." Volume 11 # - Li Page 40.

"That you may be accounted *worthy* to 'flee *out*

208

of all these things that *shall* come to pass (the Wrath of God) and to *stand before the Son of man.' "* Compare Revelation 6:17. "For the great day of His wrath is come and *who shall be able to stand?"* Who among us would dare say that the "Blessed Hope" has become the "Blasted Hope" when it is the same hope for which millions before us have gladly died! And, it becomes more blessed as the world moves nearer the Wrath of God, from which we shall escape!

A favorite saying of misguided Christians is:

> "I am not looking for the Antichrist, I am looking for Christ." To these I say "Whom shall we believe, God or man?" Paul explicitly declares two things must take place before Christ comes for the Church, the falling away, and the revealing of the Antichrist. II Thessalonians 2:3.


## The Elect

For those who may be confused as to who the "elect" are in Matthew 24:31, let the *Expository Dictionary of New Testament Words* speak again. "The word is 'Eklektos,' and means 'believers' (Jews or Gentiles), Matthew 24:22,24,31; Mark 13:20,22,27; Luke 18:7; Romans 8:33; Colossians 3:12, etc., εcc." Volume II, E Li page 21.

For each term or subject upon which I have expounded, there are many I deleted for the sake of brevity. While this treatment has not afforded me the time to sacredly deal with the four supernatural manifestations "given to me" "in visions or dreams" by night, during this study, I shall briefly divulge that the third one which came in the third month of study, long after the structure of Daniel's 70th week was revealed to me, was the personage of Jesus Christ who came to my study table, reached out to my chart of Daniel's 70th week, divided in the middle, and placed his finger on the line dividing the week and said, "You assessed it correctly, that is when I am coming." Then I responded, "But Lord, why didn't you reveal this to me weeks ago? I've spent hundreds of hours making this determination." He replied, "you could have never taught it!" It was first revealed to me through the Word, which I believed unwaveringly; then confirmed supernaturally.

• I refer you to a few simple charts that will assist you in understanding Daniel's 70th week, the last seven years of this World Order.

• Please remember as you study:

The Revelation amplifies upon and completes Daniel. Daniel saw the Seventy Sevens (a telescopic view); John saw the Seventieth Seven (a microscopic view); Daniel saw the four great empires; Babylon, Persia, Greeece, and Rome; John saw only Rome. You interpret Scripture by Scripture, Revelation by Daniel. The Bible is its own best commentary. Lay your books down and get in the Book.

## The Thessalonian Problem
### I Thessalonians

No one can begin to interpret scripture unless there is a willingness to first leave it in context where you can not manipulate it, but it can manipulate you. Jesus in Matthew 24:3 was asked these SPECIFIC QUESTIONS,

1.  "Tell us WHEN shall these things be; and

2.  "WHAT shall be the SIGN of thy coming, and

3.  "The end of the Age?"

His answers were so simply sequenced that a child could understand. Question #1 concerning the WHEN of the destruction of the Temple "when one stone would not be left upon another, and Jerusalem's house would be left desolate," He replied, "All these things shall come upon *YOU* (this generation)." Matthew 23:35-38. Some 37 to 44 years later the Roman General Titus fulfilled this prophecy.

To question #2 He answered, "Immediately after the tribulation of those days . . . THEN shall appear the SIGN of the Son of Man . . . (to) gather together His elect (saved; Christians and Jews) from the four winds . . . " Matthew 24:29 (not the coming back to earth when ALL saints are already with Him — Zechariah 14:5). If this discourse were all we had and we were willing to leave it in context, it would be sufficient for anyone to properly sequence the Lord's return.

In I Thessalonians, Paul was not endeavoring primarily to sequence the events of the Day of the Lord having not been pointedly asked as Jesus had, "When and What?" The occasion which precipitated Paul's first letter was practical first, and only incidentally eschatological. Any Bible Commentary will give the purpose of this letter. *Zondervan's Bible Dictionary states:*

211

"Some of the church members had died, causing the rest to worry whether their departed friends would share in the return of Christ" (4:13). "Still others, anticipating the Second Advent, had given up all regular employment and were idly waiting for the Lord to appear" (4:9-12). "THE EPISTLE WAS INTENDED TO ENCOURAGE THE THESSALONIAN'S GROWTH AS CHRISTIANS AND TO SETTLE THE *QUESTIONS* THAT WERE TROUBLING THEM."

It would appear the furthest thing from Paul's mind to be commenting on whether or not the Church would escape the Great Tribulation at the end of the Age; namely because the Church was in such great tribulation, that many believed they were already in it, and were overly anticipating the Lord's immediate return to rescue them out of it, and to "deliver them from the Wrath to come." I Thessalonians 1:10.

"One gets the impression that early believers identified their persecutions with the predicted period of Tribulation." *Thiessen's Lectures in Systematic Theology.*

The *AFFLICTION* they were enduring, and the ADVENT they were anticipating resulted in inordinate behavior. Increasing numbers of them, devoid of gainful employment, became idle, waiting for the Advent.

"That no man should be moved by these afflictions: for yourselves know that we are appointed thereunto. For verily, when we were with you,

we told you before that we sh[...]
tion; even as it came to pass, [...]
that ye study to be quiet, an[...]
business, and to work with [...]
we commanded you; That y[...]
toward them that are witho[...]
have lack of nothing." I Thessalonians [...]
4:11-12.

Paul's purpose was to: 1) Gently nudge them to get back to work; endure, knowing that God had not appointed them to wrath, but salvation" (I Thessalonians 5:9); 2) Encourage them to sorrow not for their deceased loved ones, because God would bring these with Him when "He descends from heaven . . . ''

The intent of this letter was to deal with a very practical and delicate problem, which if not corrected, would destroy the viability of this body of believers; not to delineate the sequential order of the Day of the Lord.

## II Thessalonians

Instead of receiving Paul's first letter in context, they, like many since, lifted out a phrase of I Thessalonians 4:15:

"This we say unto you by the word of the Lord that WE WHICH ARE ALIVE AND REMAIN UNTO THE COMING OF THE LORD shall not prevent them which are asleep."

Unfortunately, those charged with reading the letter (I Thessalonians 5:27) decided to "edit it." They taught

..., "All of *US* aren't going to die. Some of
...ng to be alive and remain until Christ comes.
... is! Paul said it was the word of the Lord to us!"
...sic text without a context — only a pretext. The
...onths following saw the same conditions Paul endeavored to correct with the first letter grow worse.
Unemployment increased, dependency accelerated;
idleness brought on gossip.

"Why build a house? We'll just get married and
live with Mom and Dad. Christ will surely come
before we could finish it. Why plant a crop this
Spring; He'll probably be back before harvest
time."

The latter state was worse than the first; which
necessitated the second letter only months after the first.

"Concerning the coming of our Lord Jesus
Christ and our being gathered together to be
with him: I beg you, brothers, do not be so easily
confused in your thinking or upset by the claim
that the Day of the Lord has come. Perhaps this
was said by someone prophesying, or by someone preaching. Or it may have been said that we
wrote this in a letter. Do not let anyone fool you
in any way. For the Day will not come until the
final Rebellion takes place and the Wicked One
appears, who is destined to hell." II Thessalonians 2:1-3 TEV.

Paul was declaring with all the emphasis he could
pen that the day of Christ to which he had referred in I
Thessalonians 4:16 could not come until two things took

place; the falling away, and the antichrist revealed.

## The "he"

"Remember ye not, that, when I was yet with you, I told you these things? And now ye know what withholdeth that he might be revealed in his time. For the mystery of iniquity doth already work: only *he* who now letteth will let, until he be taken out of the way." II Thessalonians 2:5-7.

George Milligan, in St. Paul's Epistle to the Thessalonians, said of this "he":

"It is a veiled description of the restraining power of law and order, especially as these were embodied at the time in the Roman Empire or its rulers."

James Denney in *Expositor's Bible* states:

"There is no reason to doubt that those fathers of the Church are right who identified it with the Empire of Rome and its sovereign head."

"It will be seen that opinion generally has held, that the hinderer is law and order, as represented in the Roman government and then in the governments that followed." *Thiessen's Lectures in Systematic Theology.*

"For the mystery of iniquity doth already work: only he who now letteth will let, until he be taken out of the way..." is generally understood of the Roman Power. . . . It was almost unanimous judgement of the early fathers that the obstacle to the development of Antichrist was the Roman Empire. As long as the temporal power was present, it was impossible that an ecclesiastic should become the virtual sovereign of the world." *Systematic Theology*, Charles Hodge.

The Church was already in severe persecution at the hands of Rome, so Paul chose not to invite more suffering by naming this Roman power. He had previously in person identified it. Rome was so powerful that Paul knew *another* Super World Dictator professing to be above all could not rise to power until Rome was removed. Likewise, we know this power which has prevented the revealing of the Wicked One has been subsequent government structures. When the governments of the world become unable to enforce law and order (or ''is taken out of the way''), this condition will give rise to the revelation of this Wicked One World Leader, who will himself bring about some semblance of law and order. He will be revealed to the Christians in II Thessalonians 2:3 at the outset of the last seven years, but his wickedness will not be revealed to the world until midweek.

The recent pre-trib doctrine teaches that this ''he'' is the Holy Spirit. There are many blatant inconsistencies which render this untrue. Let us look at one. If the Church is to be raptured before the Tribulation, and ''he'' the Holy Spirit is taken out at this time, as pre-trib espouses, how would those many Tribulation Saints with whom antichrist makes war

(Daniel 7:21; Revelation 13:7) get converted? The word teaches the Agency of Regeneration is the Holy Spirit. We must be born of His Spirit (Galatians 4:29); justified by the Spirit (I Timothy 3:16). There could be no tribulation saints in the absence of the Holy Spirit!

Paul firmly establishes his point in this second letter by declaring the fallacy of looking for Christ before one looks for two things which must precede Him; 1) The falling away, and 2) The antichrist revealed. It is absurd, but true, the same problem Paul endeavored to correct with this letter is still prevalent, and much of Christianity is still falsely declaring Christ could come at any moment without these two prerequisites. Small wonder that Paul prefaces this verse with: "Let no man deceive you by any means." Millions today who profess to interpret the Bible literally are as deceived as the Thessalonians because they *refuse to literally accept II Thessalonians 2:3.*

When Paul sequences the Lord's return after these two events, he then rebukes those whom he now classifies "busybodies, working not at all," foolishly waiting for the Lord's return in their lifetime; and instructs the working Christians to withdraw fellowship from those who persist in this ridiculous "idleness."

"Now we command you, brethren, in the name of our Lord Jesus Christ, that ye withdraw yourselves from every brother that walketh disorderly, and not after the tradition which he received of us. For even when we were with you, this we commanded you, that *if any would not work, neither should he eat.* For we hear that there are *some which walk among you disorderly, working not at all, but are*

217

*busybodies.* Now them that are such we command and exhort by our Lord Jesus Christ, that with quietness they work, and eat their own bread. And if any man obey not our word by this epistle, note that man, and have no company with him, that he may be ashamed." II Thessalonians 3:6-14.

### Another Misconception

Many dear Christians have erroneously taught that the apostles expected the Lord's return every day and certainly in their lifetime. Bible research indicates that they did not; especially John, Paul and Peter. For brevity's sake let's just look at Peter. Peter knew before the Lord's ascension that he would live to be an old man, then die. Jesus to Peter:

> "I tell you the truth; when you were young you used to fasten your belt and go anywhere you wanted to; but when you are old you will stretch out your hands and someone else will tie them and take you where you don't want to go." (In saying this Jesus was indicating the way in which Peter would die and bring glory to God.) John 21:18-19 *TEV.*

Peter therefore made preparation for those who would live after him by writing two epistles.

> "Therefore I intend always to remind you of these things, though you know them and are established in the truth that you have. I think it right, as long as I am in this body, to arouse you

by way of reminder, since I know that the putting off of my body will be soon, as our Lord Jesus Christ showed me. And I will see to it that after my departure you may be able at any time to recall these things." II Peter 1:12-15 *RSV*.

A minister friend asked me once, "How can we preach that people should be ready to meet the Lord any moment if the Tribulation comes first?" My reply was, "For which would you prepare your heart and soul most, if you knew that tomorrow you would 1) face possible execution, or 2) possibly meet the Lord in the air?" Another dear minister confided to me, "The Second Coming makes such a good sermon: It sounds so good to say Jesus may come today, while II Thessalonians 2:3 makes for poor preaching."

Along the way we have lost so much in the interpretation. Polycarp begged his friends in 155 A.D. not to intercede on his behalf when sentenced to be burned at the stake. He esteemed being a martyr for Christ the highest privilege.

## Finally Brethren

At the close of this study of 1978, I felt that I should write a scholarly treatise, and subsequently publish it as an addendum to Systematic Theology; Eschatology. There was no leading in this direction from the Lord, so "Mary kept these things and pondered them in her heart." I was asked to teach a course in Eschatology locally, which afforded me my first opportunity to teach these things publicly. This was followed in 1979 by a request to teach Hermeneutics (Bible Interpretation).

In January 1980, while kneeling in prayer in my bedroom, the Lord interrupted my praying, and spoke very clearly inwardly, "You are to teach 'Current Events as They Relate to Bible Prophecy.' I arose, wrote down the title as I had never heard of that phrase, per se. (Here, allow me to digress to say to those who have never experienced a supernatural manifestation from the Lord, don't despair. Start spending two hours a day in the Word [many are that devoted to television], which amounts to seven hundred and thirty hours a year; I would almost guarantee you that before the year is out, He will! Until you do this, don't criticize those who do. Many weeks I spend forty to sixty hours plus, researching the Word, but for each time the Lord supernaturally reveals something to me, I have probably spent at least five hundred hours in the Word.)

At the close of the thirteen-week course, "Current Events as They Relate to Bible Prophecy," the Lord "quickened" to me that it was now time to write. But, it was not to be written scholarly, or even systematically, but largely as I taught it here in Montgomery; that it was to be oriented toward the lay person, the businessman, and the unchurched. That these astounding Current Events on the One World Government would be the key that would arrest the attention of the lay public, so that the *truth of the last seven years would find fertile soil* in their hearts. And, as the lay persons would read and receive the truth, God would in turn reach some ministers of the Gospel. I now can see that my initial approach to do a scholarly treatise in an effort to reach the Bible Colleges and Seminaries would have never succeeded.

I have taught the Word locally, nationally, and internationally for years, and to this date, I have never received a dime in an honorarium or any money for my expenses. My lifetime pursuit of the knowledge of God through studies of His Word has been totally detached from any money motive. It is heart-rending to acknowledge that the ''Church World'' today is as encased in traditionalism as it was two thousand years ago, when Jesus came, but had to go outside the Temple and the Synagogues to choose His Disciples and reach the unreached. Indeed it was the Church people (High Priests, Pharisees and Sadducees) who crucified Him, the Living Truth. They could live with Barabbas; he was a criminal sure; but, he neither upset their tradition, nor threatened their income.

Pray for (not play with) your Pastors, Evangelists, Teachers, Ministers of Music and Education. Pray that our Churches will become more than social clubs. In October 1980, I compared Church Bulletins with the Montgomery Country Club Calendar of Events. I found the drift positively social, not spiritual. You might indicate that you are more interested in seeing the Word go forth in ''power, and in the Holy Ghost and in much assurance'' (I Thessalonians 1:5) than in having social events. You can not have both! Paul's pattern in establishing a work for God from the outset was to determine to know nothing about the people. He separated himself from the people and unto God. ''While I was with you I was determined to *know only Jesus Christ.* . . . When I spoke and preached . . . I let the Spirit and His power prove the truth to you.'' I Corinthians 2:2-4; Beck. Social activities are ''fill-ins'' necessitated by the absence

221

of the power of God. Pray that our 20th-century Shepherds might escape God's scathing reproof to an earlier group: "The diseased have ye not strengthened, neither have ye healed that which was sick, neither have ye bound up that which was broken, neither have ye brought again that which was driven away, neither have ye sought that which was lost. . . ." Ezekiel 34:4.

Christians, if you don't receive a *"love of the truth,"* not of bless me gatherings, a *"love of the truth;"* not a "love of golf;" an insatiable driving, consuming, constraining *"love of the truth,"* that will lift you above any attachment to or alignment with the teaching of men, God will send a delusion and you will believe a lie and be damned. (II Thessalonians 2:10-11.) When the first gale force winds of adversity hit, which will be National Economic Collapse, and your Gospel of prosperity fails, where will you land? The shaking has begun, and it will require tenaciously clinging to the truth (whose name is Jesus) to be able to "endure unto the end and be saved." Matthew 24:13. Nevertheless, when the Son of man comes shall He find faith on earth? Luke 18:8. As it was in Noah's day — only a few were saved! Multitudes are not going to pay the price and go in at the "catching away." Luke 14:25-33.

Only fifty percent of those who think they are saved (virgins) are going in to meet the Bridegroom! Matthew, chapter 25. Six out of the seven Churches described in Revelation which make up Christendom are in need of repentance, Jesus declared. The unpopular truth is:

> "Wide is the gate and broad is the way that leads to destruction and many there be that go in thereat: *Strait* is the gate and *narrow* is the

222

way, which leadeth unto life, and FEW there be that find it.'' Matthew 7:13-14.

The Churches are filled today with ''believe and receive'' Christians. Salvation requires more than ''Believe on the Lord Jesus Christ and thou shalt be saved.'' (Acts 16:31.) That is a classic example of lifting a text out of a context and having nothing but a pretext. Lift all other parallel passages out that refer to the Doctrine of Salvation, and apply the grand old Principle of Harmony. You will see in addition to believing, you must repent; Luke 13:3; you must come as a little child; Matthew 18:3, ''you must be born again;'' John 3:7, etc.

Oh Christians, ''Examine yourselves and see whether you be in the faith.'' II Corinthians 13:5. Many are going to be deceived. Matthew 7:22. When the Bolshevist Revolution occurred in Russia in 1917, the Russian Christian Church was in Convention in Moscow. Only six blocks from the fiercest street fighting in which hundreds were being slain, the Christian Church closed its convention in a two-day debate on whether Church Officials should wear red or yellow robes in Church functions. When the Convention adjourned, they had neither robes to wear nor churches in which to wear them. Communism had taken over. Bibles were confiscated, churches were burned, and ministers and congregations were murdered. *''They knew not what was happening until the flood came and swept them all away. That is how it will be when the Son of Man comes.''* Matthew 24:39 *TEV*.

May I ask you,

*"Have you been to Jesus*
*For the cleansing power?*
*Are you washed in the blood of the Lamb?*
*Are your garments spotless; are they white as*
  *snow?*
*Are you washed in the blood of the Lamb?"*

The time is at hand; summer is ended, harvest is past; the *day* is far spent, and the *night* is at hand. Oh, "Watchman, What of the night? What of the night? The morning cometh, but also the night!" In the natural my heart cries:

*"Wait a little longer, please Jesus,*
*There's so many still wandering out in sin;*
*Wait a little longer, please Jesus,*
*Wait until I get my loved ones in."*

But, my spirit cries, "Even so come, Lord Jesus!"

And, while we wait and "endure" the shaking process, with joy, looking for the most momentous event of all history, the coming of His Majesty, Our Most High Lord and Saviour, Jesus Christ, I commend you

". . . unto Him who is able to keep you from falling, and to present you faultless before the presence of His glory with exceeding joy; To the only wise God our Saviour, be glory and majesty, dominion and power, both now and ever. Amen." Jude 24, 25.

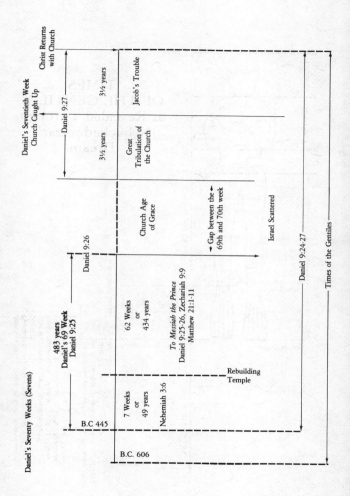

Daniel's Seventy Weeks (Sevens)

B.C. 606

B.C 445

7 Weeks
or
49 years
Nehemiah 3:6

Rebuilding
Temple

62 Weeks
or
434 years

*To Messiah the Prince*
Daniel 9:25-26, Zechariah 9:9
Matthew 21:1-11

**483 years
Daniel's 69 Week
Daniel 9:25**

Daniel 9:26

Church Age
of Grace

◄ Gap between the ►
69th and 70th week

Israel Scattered

Daniel 9:24-27

Times of the Gentiles

Daniel's Seventieth Week
Church Caught Up

Christ Returns
with Church

Daniel 9:27

3½ years

Great
Tribulation of
the Church

3½ years

Jacob's Trouble

225

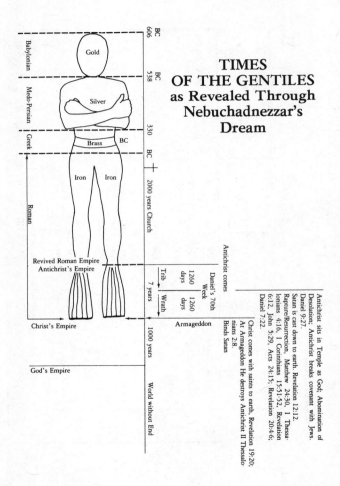

# TIMES
# OF THE GENTILES
## as Revealed Through
## Nebuchadnezzar's
## Dream

**BC 606** — Babylonian — Gold

**BC 538** — Medo-Persian — Silver

**330 BC** — Greek — Brass

**BC** — Roman — Iron | Iron

2000 years Church

Revived Roman Empire
Antichrist's Empire

Christ's Empire

God's Empire

Antichrist comes

Daniel's 70th Week

Trib — 1260 days
Wrath — 1260 days

7 years

Armageddon

1000 years

World without End

Antichrist sits in Temple as God; Abomination of Desolation; Antichrist breaks covenant with Jews. Daniel 9:27.
Satan is cast down to earth. Revelation 12:12.
Rapture/Resurrection. Matthew 24:30, 1 Thessalonians 4:16, 1 Corinthians 15:51-52. Revelation 6:12, John 5:29, Acts 24:15; Revelation 20:4-6; Daniel 7:22.

Christ comes with saints to earth. Revelation 19:20; At Armageddon He destroys Antichrist II Thessalonians 2:8.
Binds Satan

# DANIEL'S 70TH WEEK (7 YEARS)

| 1260 DAYS | 1260 DAYS | Church Removed | 1260 DAYS |
|---|---|---|---|
| **BELIEVERS** | **UNBELIEVERS** | | **UNBELIEVERS** |
| TRIBULATION | PROSPERITY | | WRATH OF GOD |

**BELIEVERS**

TRIBULATION

Antichrist revealed II Thessalonians 2:3. Great Falling Away

Gospel preached everywhere. Matthew 24:14. Antichrist makes war on and prevails against the Saints. Daniel 7:21-25

Antichrist overcomes Saints for 42 months. Revelation 13:5-7.

**UNBELIEVERS**

PROSPERITY

Peace & Safety. I Thessalonians 5:3.

Eating, drinking . . . festive mood. Marrying, buying & selling, planting, building, expecting to enjoy what has been bought, planted, and built. Luke 17:26-36.

No semblance of knowledge of impending doom.

Evil-minded men, great wickedness, corrupt earth, violence everywhere, wave of sexual perversion, irate men over suggestion of immediate doom. Genesis 6&19.

To this group, Christ comes as a thief in the night. I Thessalonians 5:2.

**UNBELIEVERS**

WRATH OF GOD

Destruction Revelation 8-20. Trumpets and Vials same, Trumpets seen from heaven, Vials seen from earth.

No Gentile saved after believers taken out in Revelation 6. They repented not: Revelation 9:20,21 & Revelation 16:9&11.

144,000 Jews sealed and protected divinely. Revelation 7&14.

One-half of one-third of Jews will go into the Thousand-Year Reign of Christ in their physical bodies to repopulate Israel. David will be their King.

TRIBULATION IS ALWAYS ON BELIEVERS, THE WRATH OF GOD IS ALWAYS ON UNBELIEVERS.

# UPDATE

Some dear people have written expressing surprise that I have labelled the usage of the digit 6 and combinations of 6 as the "666 System." Explanations have been made from officials that these just happened to be numbers designating regions, billing cycles, computer processing numbers, etc., all of which is true.

The thrust of this book, however, is to draw to the reader's attention that never before in recorded history have we witnessed the mass usage of a trio of digits (never "111," "222," etc.) until now, the time of the end, when man's number 6 emerges in a trinity, 666.

There is nothing *innately pernicious* about this number, as indeed most institutions using it have the most advanced electronic systems and should not be ostracized, but patronized, because they are more efficient. Wisdom is to be apprised that this world is being conditioned to accept a numbering system (which began in the U.S. with Social Security numbers). One day this number system will be seized by the World Dictator whose number and system will bear the entity "666." Signs of this time are everywhere.

With respect to credit cards, let me reiterate two things which I believe: 1) A card cannot be the Mark of the Beast; and 2) Christians, particularly those in business, will find it most difficult (if not impossible) to be independent of the Card segment of the Electronic Money System.

At present, I see no difference in using a number on a Credit Card, than using a number on a Social

Security Card. The Credit Card is one method of selectively *disbursing* one's earnings, which is yet voluntary; while the Social Security Card is the method by which one must *earn* his wages, and has been mandatory since 1937. Ideally, you should pay up Card purchases monthly, and strive to become debt free. I do and I am.

Soon, however, you will receive a Final Card and a Final Number. It may be called a National Identity Card, or a Registration Card, or by some other name. But, it will be the card which will be as mandatory in distributing your earnings as the Social Security Card is now in earning your wages. It will be the Card by which you both *earn* and *distribute* your income, a type of Social Security (Credit) Card.

In *U.S. News & World Report,* September 15, 1980, an article titled "A National Identity Card?" indicates the U.S. Government is contemplating issuing this all-purpose identity card, and unless an individual has such a card he will not be able to work or transact business of any kind. In the August 11, 1980, edition of *Army Times* is an article titled "Credit Card IDs for ALL: Set for 1981," which states that ". . . the cards could replace meal cards and other types of local identification. *They will be tied into a worldwide computer system* . . . according to Pentagon officials."

I believe it is safe to conjecture that the first segment of our society set to receive their Final Cards will be the U.S. Military personnel.

One much smarter than I, Dr. Patrick Fisher, Computer Scientist, says that he is prepared to return his Final Card when it arrives. As we draw near this time, I believe that each of us will be confronted with that decision.

As this edition goes to press, all 24 million citizens of South Africa have been ordered to be fingerprinted and carry ID cards in 1981; and, Mexico's President is going a step further requiring citizens and foreigners to have government-issued ID cards.

For continuous updates, we offer a Current Events/ Bible Prophecy Newsletter. See back of book.

Advertisement of a movie just released portraying the forces of evil led by Mr. "666" soon to climatically oppose the forces of God.

This book in essence is about "The Final Conflict," which will get into full sway *When Your Money Fails.* It purports to show: 1) The huge U.S. Government debt will cause the collapse of the economy; 2) Hyperinflation (resulting from the debt) will cause the demise of the dollar; 3) The emergence of a Final Card and Number (in the absence of cash) with which to conduct commerce; 5) The subsequent requirement to "mark" this number on a person's body; and, 6) The thread woven throughout this chain of events is the usage of the number "666," which characterizes the emerging One World Government System and its leader the last seven years of this World Order.

## July 1981

P.S. No, I do not have, neither have I seen, any of the checks mentioned on p.58. Yes, I do believe the sources are reliable — more reliable than the IRS. However, I predicted the "1984" aspect of this book upon what some consider a more reliable source, *The Chicago Tribune,* quoted on p.57. It's an admission by an official of the U.S. Government that "by 1984 the System will be common."

OVER

**Department of the Treasury**
**Internal Revenue Service**

# 1980

# Instructions for
# Forms W-2 and W-2P

**Box 14.—IRA codes.**—If box 9 is an IRA payment, enter <u>666</u>. Identify the kind of payment by showing one of the following code numbers after <u>666</u>: 1 for premature (other than disability or death); 2 for roll-over; 3 for disability; 4 for death; 6 for other; 7 for normal; 8 for excess contributions plus earnings on such excess contributions; and 9 for transfer to an IRA for a spouse, incident to divorce. (For example, <u>6663</u> for disability.)

When the U.S. Government uses "666" on their I.D. Badges (p.18), and on their forms (above), can the *Mark* be far behind? The one who imposes the mark will be identified by a number, "666." Revelation 13:18.

On 6-28-81, Mr. Frank Lautenberg, Chief Executive Officer of Electronic Data Processing, Inc. was asked the question on Cable News Network, "What happened to the checkless-cashless society that was supposed to arrive by 1980?" He replied, "It was delayed . . . Look for major changes in the mid 80's to bring about this paperless aspect . . . Cable TV will greatly assist it."

*This book is published by:*

Ministries, Inc.
Post Office Box 4038
Montgomery, Alabama 36104 (205) 262-4891

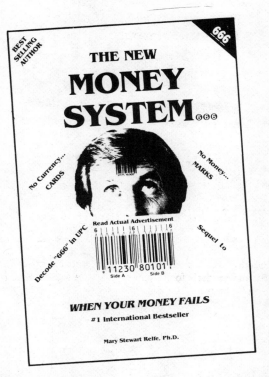

- WHEN YOUR MONEY FAILS is about the Number. THE NEW MONEY SYSTEM is about the Mark, and how the Number is incorporated into the Mark.

- The Mark, in the form of a Bar Code, will become the means of required Identification in the Cashless Society, without which no one can buy or sell.

- Those who designed the Cashless System will finally realize their ulterior motive: All the money of the world. This is the NEW MONEY SYSTEM. They will have the money; the public will have the "Marks." Then will be brought to pass the saying,

> "MONEY CAME TO PASS,
> IT DIDN'T COME TO STAY."

FOR A CONTRIBUTION OF $5.00
AT CHRISTIAN BOOKSTORES,
OR USE ORDER FORMS IN BACK

**666** BEST-SELLER

# WHEN YOUR MONEY FAILS 666

**666**

the "666 System" is here.

The Government · The Number · The Card · The Mark

RED CHINA PRODUCT LABEL

EUROPEAN PRODUCT STAMP

LEAR SIEGLER INC.
U.S. PRODUCT SEAL

Mary Stewart Relfe, Ph.D.

REVISED

UPDATED

—FOR A—
CONTRIBUTION
OF $5.00

- Best-seller in 6 weeks!

- #1 International Best-seller in 8 months!

- This book will grow more timely each year till Jesus comes!

- More current than when first published.

- EVERY CHRISTIAN HOME NEEDS ONE.

AT CHRISTIAN BOOKSTORES,
OR USE ORDER FORMS IN BACK

# ECONOMIC ADVISOR
A Newsletter on Finance, Currency and Banking,
with highlights from Bible Prophecy

*WITH GUEST WRITER*

**EDITOR:**
Mary Stewart Relfe, Ph.D.

**ASSOCIATE EDITOR:**
Bernard Stewart, B.S., M.A.

**MANAGING EDITOR:**
Sally O'Brien

**DR. C.M. WARD
PROPHECY ANALYST**

- IN-DEPTH ANALYSES of key issues, especially as these affect Economies and Currencies of the world, scrutinized in the light of Bible Prophecies.

- EXCITING UPDATES on the worldwide "666 System."

- PLUS RECOMMENDATIONS in each Newsletter on how to prepare for Economic and Monetary chaos.

- OVER 1 MILLION MAILED IN '81

- A BI-MONTHLY PUBLICATION

Some outstanding articles in 1981 issues of **Economic Advisor** Newsletter were:

*How Close Are We?* by Dr. Ward

*Bank Failures Looming in '81* by Dr. Relfe

*Why Interest Rates Will Remain High in '81* by Dr. Relfe

*The Warning of the Medfly* by Dr. Ward

*Money Market Funds — A Trap* by Dr. Relfe

*The Air Traffic Controllers' Strike* by Dr. Ward

*Moratorium on Insurance Policy Loans* by Dr. Relfe

*Are the Saudis Reversing Economic Policy?* by Dr. Ward

*Sadomasochism in Bible Prophecy* by Dr. Relfe

*Formal UN Resolution Banning Christmas* by Dr. Relfe

*Gold Is Being Remonitized Internationally (Unofficially)* by Dr. Relfe

*Social Security — Eternal Security* by Dr. Ward

*Communist Revolution in Mexico in '83?* by Dr. Relfe

*Astronomers Find Biggest Hold Ever* by Dr. Relfe

*Why Silver Will Be Scarce in '84* by Dr. Relfe

PLUS many, many more

This Newsletter is NEWS BEFORE THE NEWS!

FOR CONTRIBUTION OF $20.00
SEE ORDER FORMS ON BACK PAGES

*Published by:*
**MINISTRIES, INC.**
P.O. Box 4038
Montgomery, Alabama 36104
205/262-4891

*All contributions toward this non-profit religious ministry are tax deductible (IRS Tax #63-0810862).*

# BOOK AND NEWSLETTER ORDER FORM

UNITED KINGDOM ORDERS
SHOULD USE LAST COUPON.                                                    QTY.    AMOUNT CONTRIBUTED

**The New Money System,** © 1982, Relfe    _____    _____
**When Your Money Fails,** © 1981, Relfe    _____    _____

| Quantity prices for above two books ONLY: | 1 — $ 5.00 | 3 — $12.00 | 5 — $ 18.00 |
|---|---|---|---|
| | 10 — $35.00 | 25 — $80.00 | 50 — $150.00 |

**Economic Advisor & Bible Prophecy Newsletter,** Relfe; 1 year's subscription $20.00    _____    _____

## OTHER BOOKS * Price Each (No Quantity Discount):

| | | QTY | AMOUNT |
|---|---|---|---|
| **Christ Returns by 1988,** Deal | $5 paper | _____ | _____ |
| **New Money or None,** Cantelon | $3 paper | _____ | _____ |
| **Your Money Matters,** MacGregor | $6 paper | _____ | _____ |
| **Satan's Mark Exposed,** Kirban | $5 paper | _____ | _____ |
| **Electronic Nightmare,** Wicklein | $15 hard | _____ | _____ |
| **Trim for Him,** Cameron | $3 paper | _____ | _____ |

**TOTAL FOR BOOKS**    _____    _____
**SHIPPING AND HANDLING**    _____    _____
**TOTAL U.S. DOLLARS ENCLOSED**    _____    _____

**MINISTRIES, INC.** P.O. Box 4038, Montgomery, Alabama 36104 / (205) 262-4891

☐ Check enclosed
☐ MasterCard
☐ VISA

When using Credit Card, show number in space below.

When using MasterCard also give Interbank No. (just above your name on card)    Card Expires | Month | Year

**SIGNATURE** _____

**POSTAGE & HANDLING**

| TOTAL FOR BOOKS | Up to 5.00 | 5.01-10.00 | 10.01-20.00 | 20.01-35.00 | Over 35.00 |
|---|---|---|---|---|---|
| DELIVERY CHARGE | 1.50 | 2.00 | 2.50 | 2.95 | NO CHARGE |

SHIP TO _____
Mr. / Mrs. / Miss          (Please PRINT)

ADDRESS _____

CITY _____ STATE _____ ZIP_____

**NO DEBITS CARDS ACCEPTED**

*All contributions toward this non-profit religious ministry are tax deductible (IRS Tax #63-0810862).*

# BOOK AND NEWSLETTER ORDER FORM

*UNITED KINGDOM ORDERS*
*SHOULD USE LAST COUPON.*                                **QTY.**    **AMOUNT CONTRIBUTED**

**The New Money System,** © 1982, Relfe      _____    _____
**When Your Money Fails,** © 1981, Relfe      _____    _____

| *Quantity prices for above two books* ONLY: | 1 — $ 5.00 | 3 — $12.00 | 5 — $ 18.00 |
|---|---|---|---|
| | 10 — $35.00 | 25 — $80.00 | 50 — $150.00 |

**Economic Advisor & Bible Prophecy Newsletter,** Relfe; 1 year's subscription $20.00      _____    _____

## OTHER BOOKS * Price Each (No Quantity Discount):

| | | | |
|---|---|---|---|
| **Christ Returns by 1988,** Deal | $5 paper | _____ | _____ |
| **New Money or None,** Cantelon | $3 paper | _____ | _____ |
| **Your Money Matters,** MacGregor | $6 paper | _____ | _____ |
| **Satan's Mark Exposed,** Kirban | $5 paper | _____ | _____ |
| **Electronic Nightmare,** Wicklein | $15 hard | _____ | _____ |
| **Trim for Him,** Cameron | $3 paper | _____ | _____ |

**TOTAL FOR BOOKS**      _____    _____

**SHIPPING AND HANDLING**      _____    _____

**TOTAL U.S. DOLLARS ENCLOSED**      _____    _____

**MINISTRIES, INC.** P.O. Box 4038, Montgomery, Alabama 36104 / (205) 262-4891

☐ Check enclosed
☐ MasterCard
☐ VISA

When using Credit Card, show number in space below.

When using MasterCard also give Interbank No. (just above your name on card)

Card Expires    Month   Year

**SIGNATURE** _____

**POSTAGE & HANDLING**

| TOTAL FOR BOOKS | Up to 5.00 | 5.01-10.00 | 10.01-20.00 | 20.01-35.00 | Over 35.00 |
|---|---|---|---|---|---|
| DELIVERY CHARGE | 1.50 | 2.00 | 2.50 | 2.95 | NO CHARGE |

SHIP TO_____
  Mr. / Mrs. / Miss          (Please PRINT)

ADDRESS _____

CITY _____ STATE _____ ZIP_____

**NO DEBITS CARDS ACCEPTED**

# TAPE MINISTRY of Dr. Mary Stewart Relfe

| | QUANTITY | PER ITEM | AMOUNT |
|---|---|---|---|
| 1. BE NOT DECEIVED | | $ 5.00 | |
| 2. THE "666 SYSTEM" | | $ 5.00 | |
| 3. WHEN YOUR MONEY FAILS, WHAT THEN? | | $ 5.00 | |
| 4. MONEY & BANKING | | $ 5.00 | |
| | | Postage & Handling | $ 1.50 |
| | | **Total enclosed** | |

MINISTRIES, INC.
P.O. Box 4038
Montgomery, Alabama 36104
(205) 262-4891

NAME _____

ADDRESS _____

CITY _____ STATE _____ ZIP _____

PHONE _____

MASTERCARD NO. _____ VISA NO. _____ EXPIRATION DATE _____

Signature of applicant _____

# TAPE MINISTRY of Dr. Mary Stewart Relfe

| | QUANTITY | PER ITEM | AMOUNT |
|---|---|---|---|
| 1. BE NOT DECEIVED | | $ 5.00 | |
| 2. THE "666 SYSTEM" | | $ 5.00 | |
| 3. WHEN YOUR MONEY FAILS, WHAT THEN? | | $ 5.00 | |
| 4. MONEY & BANKING | | $ 5.00 | |
| | Postage & Handling | | $ 1.50 |
| | **Total enclosed** | | |

**MINISTRIES, INC.**
P.O. Box 4038
Montgomery, Alabama 36104
(205) 262-4891

NAME _____

ADDRESS _____

CITY _____ STATE _____ ZIP _____

PHONE _____

MASTERCARD NO. _____ VISA NO. _____ EXPIRATION DATE _____

Signature of applicant _____

# NEW RADIO CASSETTE TAPES

Current Events extemporaneously examined in the light of Bible Prophecy by a panel of three.

**Bernard Stewart, B.S., M.A.**
Publisher/Businessman

**Mary Stewart Relfe, Ph.D.**
Author/Editor

**Rev. Simon Peter Cameron**
President, New Hope Bible College
Peterhead, Scotland

*Studio quality, 30 minutes each*

*Fast breaking subjects*

**TO ORDER, CHECK BLOCK**

☐ 101 Falkland, Scotland, World Economy
☐ 103 "Christ Is Here" *(NY Times Ad)*
☐ 105 The Bar Code
☐ 107 Distress of Nations

**EACH TAPE $5.00 CONTRIBUTION**

☐ 102 Falkland, Scotland, World Economy Part II
☐ 104 National ID Card
☐ 106 Wars & Rumors of Wars
☐ 108 Electronic Funds Transfer

Enclosed is my contribution in the amount of $ _____ for _____ tape(s). _____ × $5 =

☐ Check here for SPECIAL ★ SPECIAL (All 8 tapes for $32.00)                    $32.00

Postage & Handling                    $ 1.50

Payment in U.S. Funds Only — No Foreign Currency, Please                    **TOTAL** _____

**MINISTRIES, INC.**
P.O. Box 4038
**Montgomery, Alabama 36104**
(205) 262-4891

NAME _____

ADDRESS _____

CITY _____ STATE _____ ZIP _____

PHONE _____

MASTERCARD NO. _____ VISA NO. _____

Signature of applicant _____   EXPIRATION DATE _____

# NEW RADIO CASSETTE TAPES

**Bernard Stewart, B.S., M.A.**
Publisher/Businessman

**Mary Stewart Relfe, Ph.D.**
Author/Editor

Current Events extemporaneously examined in the light of Bible Prophecy by a panel of three.

**Rev. Simon Peter Cameron**
President, New Hope Bible College
Peterhead, Scotland

*Studio quality, 30 minutes each*

*Fast breaking subjects*

**TO ORDER, CHECK BLOCK**

**EACH TAPE $5.00 CONTRIBUTION**

- ☐ 101 Falkland, Scotland, World Economy
- ☐ 102 Falkland, Scotland, World Economy Part II
- ☐ 103 "Christ Is Here" *(NY Times Ad)*
- ☐ 104 National ID Card
- ☐ 105 The Bar Code
- ☐ 106 Wars & Rumors of Wars
- ☐ 107 Distress of Nations
- ☐ 108 Electronic Funds Transfer

Enclosed is my contribution in the amount of $ _____ for _____ tape(s). _____ × $5 = _____

☐ Check here for SPECIAL ★ SPECIAL (All 8 tapes for $32.00)                    $32.00

                                                        Postage & Handling    $ 1.50

Payment in U.S. Funds Only — No Foreign Currency, Please              **TOTAL** _____

**MINISTRIES, INC.**
P.O. Box 4038
Montgomery, Alabama 36104
(205) 262-4891

NAME _____

ADDRESS _____

CITY _____ STATE _____ ZIP _____

PHONE _____

MASTERCARD NO. _____ VISA NO. _____ EXPIRATION DATE _____

Signature of applicant _____

# UNITED KINGDOM ORDER FORM
## BOOK MINISTRY of Dr. Mary Stewart Relfe

1 copy  £ 3.50 + 40p. and p. (U.K. only)

2 copies or more post free (U.K. only)

10 copies or more 1/3rd discount, post free (U.K. only)

Special price on bulk orders

Please send _____ copy(s) of **When Your Money Fails**

Please send _____ copy(s) of **The New Money System**

I enclose: **TOTAL**

NAME _____

ADDRESS _____

_____ POSTAL CODE _____

*Return order form to:*
European Distributors
New Hope Publications, Faith Acres
Peterhead, Scotland AB4 7DQ
Telephone 0779 83-251

Exciting updates
by Dr. Mary Relfe.
**Economic Advisor and
Bible Prophecy**
One of the most widely read
newsletters in USA!
1-year subscription, bi-monthly
£ 9.00 ☐ YES ☐ NO

£ _____

£ _____

£ _____

£ _____

*European mailing costs*
1 copy £ 1 p. and p.
2 copies or more
    add 50 pence per copy
10 copies or more
    1/3rd discount, plus shipping costs

# UNITED KINGDOM ORDER FORM

## BOOK MINISTRY of *Dr. Mary Stewart Relfe*

1 copy £ 3.50 + 40p p. and p. (U.K. only)

2 copies or more post free (U.K. only)

10 copies or more 1/3rd discount, post free (U.K. only)

Special price on bulk orders

Please send _____ copy(s) of **When Your Money Fails** £ _____

Please send _____ copy(s) of **The New Money System** £ _____

I enclose: **TOTAL** £ _____

NAME _____

ADDRESS _____

_____ POSTAL CODE _____

*Return order form to:*
European Distributors
New Hope Publications, Faith Acres
Peterhead, Scotland AB4 7DQ
Telephone 0779 83-251

Exciting updates
by Dr. Mary Relfe.
**Economic Advisor and
Bible Prophecy**
One of the most widely read
newsletters in USA!
1-year subscription, bi-monthly
£ 9.00 ☐ YES ☐ NO

£ _____

*European mailing costs*
1 copy £ 1 p. and p.
2 copies or more
   add 50 pence per copy
10 copies or more
   1/3rd discount, plus shipping costs